To James,
Go Heels!
Go God!
Ed McM

NORTH CAROLINA

DAILY
DEVOTIONS
FOR
DIE-HARD
FANS

TAR HEELS

NORTH CAROLINA

TAR HEELS

*To The Revs. Scott and
Mary Jane Wilson-Parsons,
who came along and changed
everything*

DAY 1

IN THE BEGINNING

Read Genesis 1, 2:1-3.

"God saw all that he had made, and it was very good" (v. 1:31).

Five boys from Charlotte "just got together one day and started it." "It" was intercollegiate basketball at UNC.

Basketball originally arrived on campus in the early 1900s "to hype student interest during the dreary winter months" and to channel their energy into something other than rowdyism. For instance, in a scene right out of *Animal House,* some students once deposited a horse into a classroom the night before classes with hopes that the horse's deposits would make the room unfit for class. The horse did his part, but the professor "calmly held his class as usual, despite all that mess." In open defiance of university rules, more than a few students "engaged in nightly foot races with pursuing, panting faculty members."

For several years, the game lacked any formal structure at UNC. In 1910, five Charlotte students – Marvin Ritch, Cyrus Long, Bill Tillett, Junius Smith, and Roy McKnight – received permission to schedule some games with other colleges. Their coach was Nat Cartmell, the school's track coach; the athletic association was so deep in debt it couldn't afford to hire a separate coach.

Fittingly, UNC's first game was a win; the novices beat Virginia Christian 42-21 on Feb. 3, 1911. They finished with a 7-4 record that inaugural season despite having to practice outdoors for a while because the director of the school gym didn't want his floor messed up. The basketball players pressured the school administration until they were allowed indoors, which didn't help a whole lot since the building was configured for track.

The sport wasn't exactly received with "a raging fever" by the student body or by the larger community. "There wasn't much enthusiasm for basketball then," McKnight recalled. "If we had 35 or 40 people out to see games in those days, it was pretty good."

It was a beginning, though, and the rest is history.

Beginnings are important, but what we make of them is even more important. Consider, for example, how far the North Carolina men's basketball program has come since that first season. Every morning, you get a gift from God: a new beginning. God hands to you as an expression of divine love a new day full of promise and the chance to right the wrongs in your life. You can use the day to pay a debt, start a new relationship, replace a burned-out light bulb, tell your family you love them, chase a dream, solve a nagging problem . . . or not.

God simply provides the gift. How you use it is up to you. People often talk wistfully about starting over or making a new beginning. God gives you the chance with the dawning of every new day. You have the chance today to make things right – and that includes your relationship with God.

The most important key to achieving great success is to decide upon your goal and launch, get started, take action, move.
-- Legendary UCLA basketball coach John Wooden

**Every day is not just a dawn;
it is a precious chance to start over or begin anew.**

THE FAME GAME

Read 1 Kings 10:1-10, 18-29.

"King Solomon was greater in riches and wisdom than all the other kings of the earth. The whole world sought audience with Solomon" (vv. 23-24).

Charlie "Choo Choo" Justice was so famous when he played at UNC that the post office would deliver to him mail addressed simply "Choo Choo, NC."

Justice remains the greatest and most famous football player in Tar Heel history. "He was a bonafide superstar . . . a hero . . . a legend in his own time." Justice played halfback from 1946-49 and led the Heels to three major bowl games, the first in school history, and a 32-7-2 record. He was All-America in 1948-49, runner-up for the Heisman Trophy both seasons, and the 1948 National Player of the Year. His school total offense record of 4,883 yards stood until quarterback Jason Stanicek broke it in 1994.

Justice's fame rivaled that of today's movie and music stars. Hundreds of babies were named for him. The legendary Benny Goodman recorded a song "All the Way Choo Choo" that sold 50,000 copies. When a North Carolina high-school class was asked to name the greatest American, five named Dwight Eisenhower, two named Robert E. Lee, and the other 58 named Justice.

Irv Holdash, an All-American center on the Justice teams, remembered that "women, young and old, all sorts and varieties, just fawned over him and wanted to touch him." Ernie Williamson, a lineman, said, "Charlie did not have any private life at all. . . . He could not walk uptown without being completely mobbed."

Through all the fame and adulation, Justice remained "a friendly country boy who preferred the role of football player to celebrity."

Have you ever wanted to be famous? Hanging out with other rich and famous people, having folks with microphones listen to what you say, throwing money around like toilet paper, meeting adoring and clamoring fans, signing autographs, and posing for the paparazzi before you climb into your imported sports car?

Many of us yearn to be famous, well-known in the places and by the people that we believe matter. That's all fame amounts to: strangers knowing your name and your face.

The truth is that you are already famous where it really does matter, which excludes TV's talking heads, screaming teenagers, moviegoers, or D.C. power brokers. You are famous because Almighty God knows your name, your face, and everything about you.

If a persistent photographer snapped you pondering this fame – the only kind that has eternal significance – would the picture show the world unbridled joy or the shell-shocked expression of a mug shot?

Fame is strange. Once you get it, your life is never your own.
-- Charlie Justice

You're already famous because God knows your name and your face, which may be either reassuring or terrifying.

DAY 3

UNEXPECTEDLY

Read Luke 2:1-20.

"She gave birth to her firstborn, a son. She wrapped him in cloths and placed him in a manger, because there was no room for them in the inn" (v. 7).

Three of UNC's men's lacrosse national titles weren't really big surprises, but that other one was totally unexpected.

In 1981, the Heels were undefeated and ranked No. 2 entering the NCAA Tournament. They coasted past Syracuse and Navy before edging three-time defending champion Johns Hopkins in a 14-13 thriller. The 1982 season was virtually a repeat of 1981. Again, UNC went undefeated during the regular season and then routed Navy and Cornell to face Johns Hopkins for the title. Defenses dominated behind some brilliant goalkeeping by Tom Sears, the national player of the year. Only junior attackman David Wingate was unstoppable; he scored five goals to lead UNC to a 7-5 win and the national championship.

The 1991 team also sailed into the tournament unbeaten. UNC beat Loyola 11-9 in the tourney opener and then handed Syracuse its first NCAA home playoff loss in history with a 19-13 rout. The Tar Heels then whipped surprising Towson 18-13 for the title.

In each of those years, UNC was among the favorites to claim the crown. 1986 was a totally different story, though. The Heels were seeded fifth in the tournament. No team seeded lower than fourth had ever even made the championship game, and none seeded lower than third had ever won the title.

North Carolina pulled it off, though. The Tar Heels whipped Maryland 12-10 to gain a berth in the first-ever NCAA Final Four and then stunned two-time defending NCAA champion Johns Hopkins 10-9 in overtime on senior Mike Tummillo's goal off a Gary Seivold assist. In another 10-9 overtime thriller, UNC edged Virginia on an unassisted goal by Seivold to unexpectedly claim the national championship.

We think we've got everything figured out and planned for, and then something unexpected happens like UNC in 1986. Someone gets ill; you fall in love; you lose your job; you're going to have another child. Life surprises us with its bizarre twists and turns.

God is that way too, catching us unawares to remind us he's still around. A friend who hears you're down and stops by, a child's laugh, an achingly beautiful sunset -- unexpected moments of love and beauty. God is like that, always doing something in our lives we didn't expect.

But why shouldn't he? There is nothing God can't do. The only factor limiting what God can do is the paucity of our own faith.

We should expect the unexpected from God, this same deity who unexpectedly came to live among us as a man. He does, by the way, expect a response from you.

Sports is about adapting to the unexpected and being able to modify plans at the last minute.
— Sir Roger Bannister, first-ever sub-four-minute miler

God does the unexpected to remind you
of his presence -- like showing up as Jesus –
and now he expects a response from you.

DAY 4

TEARS TO TRIUMPH

Read Matthew 27:45-50, 55-61.

"Many women were there, watching from a distance. They had followed Jesus from Galilee to care for his needs" (v. 55).

It began with the tears of a loss so devastating that Coach Roy Williams said it would haunt him forever. It ended with the triumph of a national championship.

On April 5, 2008, the Tar Heels lost to Kansas 84-66 in the NCAA semifinals after trailing 40-12 early in the game. In addition to Williams' devastation, forward Tyler Hansbrough wouldn't watch the tape of the game and point guard Ty Lawson said it was the worst game of his life.

From those ashes, though, rose the 2008-09 season and the school's fifth national championship. When Hansbrough, Lawson, Wayne Ellington, and Danny Green all chose to return to Chapel Hill rather than turn pro, the media – apparently dismissing the fact that the games still had to be played -- immediately handed the title to UNC.

The players took nothing for granted, though, heading into the weight room with a vengeance during the off-season. The season had its rough spots as they all do. Senior Marcus Ginyard, the team's best defender, underwent surgery for a stress fracture. Freshman Tyler Zeller missed 13 weeks with a broken wrist. Hansbrough and Lawson missed games with injuries.

Through it all, however, the team faced up to the pressure and flourished. Then on April 6, 2009, in Detroit, the Tar Heels dismantled the Michigan State Spartans 89-72. North Carolina led by 16 points before the game was seven minutes old, "a ruthless assault that transformed the rest of the game into a formality."

Before the game, Coach Roy Williams told his team, "Invest everything. Don't come back in here with anything left." What they came back with was a national championship, the long trip from tears to triumph completed.

We all have times of defeat and loss in our lives; even the Tar Heels lose basketball games. Nothing, however, fills us with such an overwhelming sense of helplessness as the death of a loved one. There's absolutely nothing we can do about it. Like the women who stood at a distance and watched Jesus die on the darkest, bleakest day in history, we, too, can only stand helpless and weep as something precious and beautiful leaves our lives.

For the believer in Jesus Christ and his loved ones, though, the Sunday of resurrection – the grandest, most triumphant day in history – follows the Friday of death. Faith in Jesus transforms loss into triumph, not only for the loved one but for those left behind. Amid our tears and our sense of loss, we celebrate the ultimate victory of our family member or friend. Amid death, we find life; amid sorrow, we find hope.

What a way to die! What a way to live!

Remember what happened last year.
– Senior guard Bobby Frasor's speech before the 2009 semifinals

Faith in Jesus Christ transforms death
from the ultimate defeat to the ultimate victory.

LESSONS LEARNED

Read Matthew 11:20-30.

"Take my yoke upon you and learn from me" (v. 29).

Mitch Kupchak learned his lessons well enough as a student-athlete at UNC to make the Dean's List and eventually earn a masters from UCLA. Some of his most valuable lessons, though, didn't come from the classroom.

In 1972, with the rule changed, Kupchak became the first freshman ever to play varsity basketball for Dean Smith. As a senior in 1976, he was All-America and the ACC Player of the Year when he averaged 17.6 points and 11.3 rebounds per game. He went on to a ten-year career in the NBA and became the general manager of the Los Angeles Lakers in 2000. In that position, he achieved some notoriety by firing (and subsequently rehiring) Phil Jackson and by trading Shaquille O'Neal. Among the coaches he sought after he let Jackson go in 2004 were Roy Williams and Mike Krzyzewski.

Kupchak learned much about his rough-and-tumble job while he was the assistant general manager to the legendary Jerry West. However, when he first showed up in Los Angeles, he brought with him much he had learned back east in Carolina.

For instance, he learned the value of always speaking the truth. On a recruiting visit, Smith frankly told Kupchak and his parents that he would guarantee Kupchak would graduate but whether he would play or not depended upon how hard he worked. "That struck me," Kupchak remembered. "That set [Coach Smith] apart from the rest."

He learned other lessons from his time at Chapel Hill. "I have a great take on what integrity is," he said. "I understand what it is to be a professional. I appreciate relationships with people. All that started at Carolina."

Lessons learned.

Learning about anything in life requires a combination of education and experience. Education is the accumulation of facts that we call knowledge; experience is the acquisition of wisdom and discernment, which add purpose and understanding to our knowledge.

The most difficult way to learn is trial and error: dive in blindly and mess up. The best way to learn is through example coupled with a set of instructions: Someone has gone ahead to show you the way and has written down all the information you need to follow.

In teaching us the way to live godly lives, God chose the latter method. He set down in his book the habits, actions, and attitudes that make for a way of life in accordance with his wishes. He also sent us Jesus to explain and to illustrate.

God teaches us not just how to exist but how to live. We just need to be attentive students.

It's what you learn after you know it all that counts.

— *John Wooden*

To learn from Jesus is to learn what life is all about and how God means for us to live it.

DAY 6

MIRACLE PLAY

Read Matthew 12:38-42.

"He answered, 'A wicked and adulterous generation asks for a miraculous sign!'" (v. 39)

The player who made the most miraculous shot in Tar Heel women's basketball history didn't even see it fall.

Charlotte Smith is one of the most decorated players in UNC basketball history. She was ESPN's National Player of the Year for the 1993-94 season and a first-team All America in 1994-95. That senior season she led the ACC in scoring and rebounding. She was the ACC Rookie of the Year in 1992 and was both All-ACC and ACC Tournament MVP as a junior and as a senior. Her number 23 was the first ever retired for a Tar Heel women's basketball player.

Smith's moment of immortal glory for Tar Heel fans came in the finals of the 1994 NCAA title game. The game appeared over; Louisiana Tech would win 59-57. After all the clock showed a ridiculous 0:00.7 left. But after two time outs, Stephanie Lawrence inbounded the ball to Smith on the right wing; she immediately let fly and drilled a three-pointer that propelled the Tar Heels to the championship.

"I didn't look at it," Smith said of her miraculous shot. "And the mob got me before I knew it had gone in." The "mob" was her teammates, who rushed onto the floor and buried her in jubilation. Smith had to wait and watch the replay to see the shot heard round the world – or at least round the Tar Heel nation. Perhaps forgotten in all the excitement over *the* shot was that Smith, who led Carolina in rebounds all four seasons, hauled down a career-high 23 rebounds against Louisiana Tech, setting an NCAA championship game record.

Never to be forgotten, though, is her miraculous shot.

Miracles – like Charlotte Smith's game-winning shot with no time left -- defy rational explanation. Escaping with minor abrasions from an accident that totals your car is another good example. As is recovering from an illness that seemed terminal. Underlying the notion of miracles is that they are rare instances of direct divine intervention that reveal God.

But life shows us quite the contrary, that miracles are anything but rare. Since God made the world and everything in it, everything around you is miraculous. Even you are a miracle.

Your life can be mundane, dull, and ordinary, or it can be spent in a glorious attitude of childlike wonder and awe. It depends on whether or not you see the world through the eyes of faith. Only through faith can you discern the hand of God in any event; only through faith can you see the miraculous and thus see God.

Jesus knew that miracles don't produce faith, but rather faith produces miracles.

Do you believe in miracles? Yes!
— Broadcaster Al Michaels when U.S. defeated USSR in hockey
in 1980 Winter Games.

Miracles are all around us,
but it takes the eyes of faith to see them.

DAY 7

YOU CHOOSE

Read Deuteronomy 30:15-20.

"I have set before you life and death, blessings and curses.
Now choose life, so that you and your children may live"
(v. 19).

Julius Peppers had a choice to make.

His dreams were "wrapped up in basketball." His talents, though, pushed him toward football.

Peppers was so good at both sports in high school that he had his own mail slot in the school office to handle all the recruiting letters he received. He accepted a football scholarship to UNC with the understanding he could walk on to the basketball team.

After a redshirt season, in 1999 Peppers led the Heels in tackles for loss and sacks. He then became the basketball team's sixth man, helping UNC advance to the Final Four. "Julius was a godsend, the missing piece for us," Coach Bill Guthridge said.

As a sophomore defensive end, Peppers led the nation with fifteen sacks. He then returned to the basketball team again as the sixth man. When the season ended, though, to his surprise Peppers found himself looking forward to football. Without his realizing it, football had become his first love.

So he had a choice: Did he keep on playing two sports or did he commit totally to football, knowing that he was giving up basketball forever? Peppers chose: He would stay at Chapel Hill one more season and he would not play basketball.

In 2001, Peppers was All-America and All-ACC. He won the Chuck Bednarik Award as the nation's top defensive player, the Lombardi Award as the best collegiate lineman in the country, and the Bill Willis Trophy as the nation's best defensive lineman. John Bunting's Heels went 8-5 and whipped Auburn in the Peach Bowl. Peppers was the second pick in the 2002 draft, was the NFL Defensive Rookie of the Year, and went on to an All-Pro career.

Julius Peppers made the right choice.

Your life is the sum of the choices you've made just as Julius Peppers' is today. That is, you have arrived at this moment and this place in your life because of the choices you made in your past. Your love of the Tar Heels. Your spouse or the absence of one. Mechanic, teacher, or beautician. Condo in downtown Charlotte or ranch home in Greenville. Dog, cat, or goldfish. You chose; you live with the results.

That includes the most important choice you will ever have to make: faith or the lack of it. That we have the ability to make decisions when faced with alternatives is a gift from God, who allows that faculty even when he's part of the choice. We can choose whether or not we will love him. God does remind us that this particular choice has rather extreme consequences: Choosing God's way is life; choosing against him is death.

Life or death. What choice is that?

The choices you make in life make you.

-- *John Wooden*

God gives you the freedom to choose: life or death; what kind of choice is that?

DAY 8

HEAD GAMES

Read Job 28.

"The fear of the Lord -- that is wisdom, and to shun evil is understanding" (v. 28).

Known for his exceptionally ferocious dunks, James Worthy even dunked one off an opposing player's head in the finals of the 1982 NCAA Tournament.

Jimmy Black, the starting point guard and a co-captain of the '82 national champions, flatly declared that Worthy was the team's best player. Worthy left UNC as a junior after the '82 season, and in 2003 he became the first player on the team to reach the Basketball Hall of Fame. He was first-team All-America and the national Player of the Year in '82.

Worthy's specialty was crowd-pleasing, thunderous dunks. As Black put it, Worthy "wasn't looking for style points as much as he was looking to put a dent in the floor." In the national semifinal win over Houston, Worthy had a dunk out of the Four Corners in which Black said he "took off from [the] foul line and absolutely tomahawked the ball through about three of Houston's players." *Sports Illustrated* called it a "sledgehammer slam," and said, "Dr. J, move over for Dr. James."

Worthy had an even more memorable dunk in the national championship win over Georgetown, one of five he had for the game. Black recalled that the Heels trailed 49-45 in the last half when Buzz Peterson stole the ball and flipped it ahead to Worthy, who was one-on-one with Sleepy Floyd, a first-team All-America. As Floyd jumped to try and block the dunk, Worthy slammed it through the goal. The ball burst through the net and hit Floyd in the forehead. To make the play even more ignominious for Floyd, he was called for a foul.

Senior Chris Burst said, "That was one of my favorite moments of the game – seeing James dunk on Sleepy Floyd's head."

You're a thinking person. When you talk about using your head, you're not speaking of anything remotely similar to how Sleepy Floyd used his head against James Worthy's dunk. Logic and reason are part of your psyche. A coach's bad call frustrates you and your children's inexplicable behavior flummoxes you. Why can't people just think things through?

That goes for matters of faith too. Jesus doesn't tell you to turn your brain off when you walk into a church or open the Bible. In fact, when you seek Jesus, you seek him heart, soul, body, and mind. The mind of the master should be the master of your mind so that you consider every situation in your life through the critical lens of the mind of Christ. With your head *and* your heart, you encounter God, who is, after all, the true source of wisdom.

To know Jesus is not to stop thinking; it is to start thinking divinely.

Football is more mental than physical, no matter how it looks from the stands.

-- *Pro Hall-of-Fame linebacker Ray Nitschke*

**Since God is the source of all wisdom,
it's only logical that you encounter him
with your mind as well as with your emotions.**

DAY 9

BE PREPARED

Read Matthew 10:5-23.

"I am sending you out like sheep among wolves. Therefore be as shrewd as snakes and as innocent as doves" (v. 16).

The undefeated national championship team of 1956-57 was one of the most talented in Carolina history, but they didn't win by just showing up. They showed up prepared.

The roster included Lennie Rosenbluth, the conference and national Player of the Year in 1957; Pete Brennan, the ACC Player of the Year in '58 and a two-time All-America; and Tommy Kearns, second team All-America and twice All-ACC.

Fourteen of their 32 wins were by ten points or fewer; they needed three overtimes to beat Michigan State in the semis and three more to beat the heavily favored Kansas Jayhawks with Wilt Chamberlain in the finals. Preparation made the difference.

Head coach Frank McGuire "prepared his players for all eventualities on a basketball court." "We applied theoretical situations in practice-game sessions," he said. For instance, McGuire would holler to his players, "A minute to play. You're four points ahead." The task was to protect the lead. Or "A minute to play. You're four points behind." The task was to press and win.

Every Tar Heel game was filmed, and files were kept on each upcoming opponent. "We saved every observation, every newspaper clipping, or comment," McGuire said. "We saved brochures. During games our student manager sat next to me on the bench and recorded all the comments I made. That went into the file as well." Before each game, the coaches compiled the information, and the players received it in two-hour blackboard sessions.

The Heels were so well prepared for any eventuality that they went right on and beat Kansas for the national championship even though Rosenbluth fouled out in regulation.

You know the importance of preparation in your own life. You went to the bank for a car loan, facts and figures in hand. That presentation you made at work was seamless because you practiced. The kids' school play suffered no meltdowns because they rehearsed. Knowing what you need to do and doing what you must to succeed isn't luck; it's preparation.

Jesus understood this, and he prepared his followers by lecturing them and by sending them on field trips. Two thousand years later, the life of faith requires similar training and study. You prepare so you'll be ready when that unsaved neighbor standing beside you at your backyard grill asks about Jesus. You prepare so you will know how God wants you to live. You prepare so you are certain in what you believe when the secular, godless world challenges it.

And one day you'll see God face to face. You certainly want to be prepared for that.

Spectacular achievements are always preceded by unspectacular preparation.

-- Roger Staubach

**Living in faith requires constant study
and training, preparation for the day
when you meet God face to face.**

DAY 10

HOME IMPROVEMENT

Read Ephesians 4:7-16.

"The body of Christ may be built up until we all reach unity in the faith and in the knowledge of the Son of God and become mature, attaining to the whole measure of the fullness of Christ" (vv. 12b, 13).

Once upon a time there was only an open field.

UNC's earliest home football games – sixty or so of them over twenty-seven seasons – were played on a field just east of Bynum Hall. Wooden stands for baseball were erected at the field around 1884; those stands burned in 1909.

In 1914, Isaac Edward Emerson, an 1879 UNC graduate and the inventor of Bromo-Seltzer, donated $26,000 to the university for the construction of an athletic field for baseball and football. On the site of what is now Davis Library and the Student Union, Emerson Field opened in 1916. Edward Reid played fullback on Emerson and remembered that the field wasn't level. "Down in one corner it was maybe two feet lower than the rest of the field," Reid said. "I remember I always hated to punt from that low corner. You felt like you were punting uphill."

Emerson was designed to seat 2,400, and even with the addition of some wooden bleachers, by 1921 the university was turning away thousands of paying customers. Expansion would ruin the site for baseball, so the decision was made to build a new stadium, the construction to be funded from alumni donations.

Fundraising didn't go too well until William Rand Kenan, Jr. (class of 1894) volunteered to cover the entire cost as a memorial to his parents. Kenan Stadium (capacity 24,000) opened on Nov. 12, 1927, with a 27-0 win over Davidson College. Edison Foard scored the first touchdown.

The facility has subsequently undergone a number of renovations and expansions, earning it the quite truthful designation of "America's Most Beautiful Stadium."

No matter how beautiful it is, Kenan Stadium will always be subject to improvement. It's the same way in your life. You try to improve at whatever you tackle. You attend training sessions and seminars to do your job better. You take golf or tennis lessons and practice to get better. You play that new video game until you master it. To get better at anything requires a dedication involving practice, training, study, and preparation.

Your faith life is no different. Jesus calls us to improve ourselves spiritually by becoming more mature in our faith. We can always know more about God's word, discover more ways to serve God, deepen our prayer life and our trust in God, and do a better job of being Jesus to other people through simple acts of kindness and caring. In other words, we can always become more like Jesus.

One day we will all stand before God as finished products. We certainly want to present him a mature dwelling, a spiritual mansion, not a hovel.

I was not prepared to find the stadium as beautiful as it is.
-- William Rand Kenan, Jr. upon his first inspection of Kenan Stadium

**Spiritual improvement means a constant effort
to become more like Jesus in our day-to-day lives.**

DAY 11

GLORY DAYS

Read Colossians 3:1-4.

"When Christ, who is your life, appears, then you also will appear with him in glory" (v. 4).

Chris Watson had his moment of glory.

On their way to a 10-2 season, the Tar Heels buried Wake Forest 45-6 on Oct. 5, 1996. The game was the routine blowout that everyone expected. For Watson, though, the game was the most exciting one of his career. He scored his first-ever collegiate touchdown.

Watson lettered four years and started three years. Until that momentous evening, though, he had never scored a touchdown. When he did, he thoroughly enjoyed the moment of glory. Watson bulled his way in from the one and promptly "went into a maniacal, slobbering, gonzo delirium. He bumped chests with teammates, shook like a leaf, hugged everyone in sight, high-fived the ones he didn't grab and received a hundred pats on the helmet."

"I'm not sure I've ever seen a kid more excited," said head coach Mack Brown. "You don't understand," Watson said in explaining his over-the-top end-zone dance. "I've been waiting FOUR YEARS." In fact, when Brown sent Watson in with the play up the gut, the fullback told his teammates, "Don't be surprised if I get a 15-yarder [for celebrating]."

Brown said he was sure folks at the game were wondering what the big deal was about a one-yard run in a lopsided game.

He pointed out that Watson spent most of his days blocking for tailback Leon Johnson, who in the same game set a UNC record for career points.

At practice the Tuesday after the game, Brown teasingly told Watson he probably had his sights set on Johnson's scoring record. Watson just smiled; he had his moment of glory.

You may well remember the play that was your moment of athletic glory. Or the night you received an award from a civic group for your hard work. Your first (and last?) ace on the golf course. Your promotion at work. Your first-ever 10K race. Life does have its moments of glory.

But they amount to a lesser, transient glory, which actually bears pain with it since you cannot recapture the moment. The excitement, the joy, the happiness – they are fleeting; they pass as quickly as they arose, and you can never experience them again.

Glory days that last forever are found only through Jesus. That's because true glory properly belongs only to God, who has shown us his glory in Jesus. To accept Jesus into our lives is thus to take God's glory into ourselves. Glory therefore is an ongoing attribute of Christians. Our glory days are right now, and they will become even more glorious when Jesus returns.

The real glory is being knocked to your knees and then coming back. That's real glory. That's the essence of it.
> -- *Vince Lombardi*

**The glory of this earth is fleeting,
but the glory we find in Jesus lasts forever
– and will only get even more magnificent.**

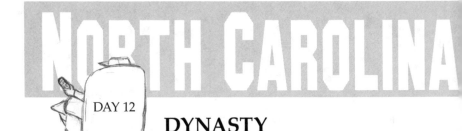

DAY 12

DYNASTY

Read 2 Samuel 7:8-17.

"Your house and your kingdom will endure forever before me; your throne will be established forever" (v. 16).

The North Carolina women's soccer team is the greatest college sports dynasty ever. No less an expert than *Sports Illustrated* has declared it "definitely" to be so.

And that was in 2003. Much has happened since then: mainly more wins at a downright embarrassing pace and more national championships. Under the direction of Coach Anson Dorrance, the Tar Heels "have hoarded national and conference championships at a stupendous rate, compiled an overall record staggering in its numerical verity, established records likely never to be approached again and procured the respect befitting a dynasty."

The numbers don't lie.

The national championship in 2009 was the program's 21st including one in the old AIAW, which governed women's athletics before the NCAA. No other school has won more than two titles. The Heels have won 20 of the 22 ACC tournament championships; the two losses came in overtime shootouts. After 31 seasons through 2009, the record was 696-36-21, a winning percentage that no other program at any other college can come close to.

From the season opener in 1986 into the 1990 season, the Tar Heels went an NCAA-record 103 matches without a loss, winning 97 of them. They followed that with another NCAA record, 92 wins in a row. Only three UNC teams in history have lost more than two matches in a season, and the 21-3 team of 1990 won the national championship. Among the NCAA records the Tar Heels have set in addition to the two streaks mentioned above are 84 consecutive conference home wins, 55 consecutive conference wins, and most wins in a season (27 three times).

The Tar Heels are way beyond good; they are dynastic.

No matter how dominating they are, though, UNC's women's soccer team doesn't win every NCAA championship. History teaches us that kingdoms, empires, countries, and even sports programs rise and fall. Dynasties end as events and circumstances conspire and align to snap all winning streaks.

Your life is like that; you win some and lose some. You get a promotion on Monday and your son gets arrested on Friday. You breeze through your annual physical but your dog dies. You finally line up a date with that cutie next door and get sent out of town on business.

Only one dynasty will never end because it is based upon an everlasting promise from God. God promised David the king an enduring line in the appearance of one who would establish God's kingdom forever. That one is Jesus Christ, the reigning king of God's eternal and unending dynasty. The only way to lose out on that one is to stand on the sidelines and not get in the game.

UNC is not a basketball school but a women's soccer school.
-- Dean Smith

All dynasties and win streaks end
except the one God established with Jesus as its
king; this one never loses and never will.

DAY 13

IN THE BAD TIMES

Read Philippians 1:3-14.

"What has happened to me has really served to advance the gospel. . . . Because of my chains, most of the brothers in the Lord have been encouraged to speak the word of God more courageously and fearlessly" (vv. 12, 14).

As a two-time All-America on the basketball court, Al Wood has known the good times. Off the court, though, he has also known the bad times.

Wood's signature moment in Carolina history came in 1981, his senior season, when he led UNC to the national finals by pouring in 39 points against Virginia and Ralph Sampson in the NCAA semifinals. That evening back in Chapel Hill, joyous Heel fans painted "Al Wood 39" all over Franklin Street. Wood was on top of the world.

He hadn't always been. As a child, his home situation was so unstable that his grandmother adopted him. His father wasn't around, and his mother was an alcoholic who spent years in prison after killing the man she lived with in an alcohol-fueled rage she didn't even recall. She died in 2004.

When Wood's NBA career ended in 1986, the bad times returned. "He had money, plenty of free time, and no real purpose in life. His life started spiraling downhill" from drinking and gambling.

In 1989, Wood took a harsh look at his destructive behavior and turned to the Bible for inspiration and the power to change.

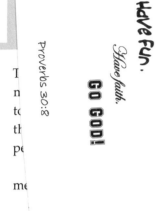

Proverbs 30:8

Have faith.
GO GOD!

Have Fun.

T... lcohol moved out. He became a
n... ng his own story as a testament
t... nge lives. "The most gratifying
th... ut something in me that allows
pe... about God's love," Wood said.
... times, Wood knows he "was
me... else."
... d. Your biopsy looks cancerous.
You... affair. As Al Wood's life and
test......y illustrate, hard, tragic times are as much a part of life
as are breathing, income tax returns, and lousy television shows.

This applies to Christians too. Faith in Jesus Christ does not
exempt anyone from pain. Jesus promises he will be there for us
to lead us through the valleys; he never promises that we will not
enter them.

The question thus becomes how you handle the bad times. You
can buckle to your knees in despair and cry, "Why me?" Or you
can hit your knees in prayer and ask, "What do I do with this?"

Setbacks and tragedies are opportunities to reveal and to
develop true character and abiding faith. Your faithfulness -- not
your skipping merrily along through life without pain -- is what
reveals the depth of your love for God.

*If I were to say, "God, why me?" about the bad things, then I should
say, "God, why me?" about the good things that happened in my life.*
— Arthur Ashe

**Faithfulness to God requires faith even in --
especially in -- the bad times.**

DAY 14

A SECOND CHANCE

Read John 7:53-8:11.

*"'Then neither do I condemn you,' Jesus declared. 'Go
now and leave your life of sin'" (v. 8:11).*

The Duke players had already doused their head coach so sure
were they of the win. All the Heels wanted was a second chance.

UNC's 2007 football season, the initial campaign under Butch
Davis, was one long gut-wrenching experience after another. Six
times the Tar Heels lost by seven points or fewer. In the season
finale on Nov. 24, the heartache seemed destined to continue.

A 9-yard pass from T.J. Yates to Brandon Tate staked the Heels
to an early 7-0 lead, but Duke led 14-7 in the fourth quarter until
the Heels got a 7-yard TD run from freshman tailback Greg
Little. With 4:06 left, the game was tied. The score amounted to
some personal redemption for Little, who earlier in the game had
drawn an unsportsmanlike conduct penalty that stymied a Tar
Heel drive. He went up to Davis on the sideline and asked for a
second chance: "Coach, you give me the opportunity, I will help
us win this game."

The Blue Devils responded to the late UNC touchdown with
a drive of their own and huddled up with only one second left,
getting set for the game-winning 40-yard field goal. Sure of the
win, the excited Duke players gave their coach a water-bucket
bath on the sideline. Across the field, the UNC players could only
wait and hope for overtime and a second chance.

The Heels got their second chance when the kick sailed wide left. Duke then missed a second field-goal try on the opening possession of the overtime. On the sideline, tired but determined to make the most of the team's and his second chance, Little suggested a play. The Heels ran it to perfection. Bobby Rome and Aaron Stahl laid down their blocks, and Little hit the hole and scampered 25 yards for a touchdown.

The second-chance Heels had a 20-14 win.

"If I just had a second chance, I know I could make it work out." Ever said that? If only you could go back and tell your dad one last time you love him, take that job you passed up rather than relocate, or replace those angry shouts at your son with gentle encouragement. If only you had a second chance, a mulligan.

As the story of Jesus' encounter with the adulterous woman illustrates, with God you always get a second chance. No matter how many mistakes you make, God will never give up on you. Nothing you can do puts you beyond God's saving power. You always have a second chance because with God your future is not determined by your past or who you used to be. It is determined by your relationship with God through Jesus Christ.

God is ready and willing to give you a second chance – or a third chance or a fourth chance – if you will give him a chance.

I have to thank God for giving me the gift that he did as well as a second chance for a better life.
-- Olympic figure skating champion Oksana Baiul

You get a second chance with God
if you give him a chance.

DAY 15

PLAN AHEAD

Read Psalm 33:1-15.

"The plans of the Lord stand firm forever, the purposes of his heart through all generations" (v. 11).

UNC had just been waxed by Indiana, and more of the same seemed on the way when the Heels pulled into Lexington on Dec. 17, 1962, to take on Kentucky. Dean Smith had a plan, though.

Smith's second-ever team walked into Kentucky's massive arena with eyes wide and jaws dropped. Starter Charlie Shaffer recalled looking around at the packed, screaming crowd and wondering out loud, "What have we got ourselves into?" Senior point guard Larry Brown broke out into hives in the locker room.

Smith knew his team was intimidated, so he told them to pretend they were playing Tennessee. Then he reviewed his plan. Senior Yogi Poteet was to shadow Kentucky's Cotton Nash, the best collegiate player in the country. Then if UNC got the lead, they would try something that had worked in practice.

Carolina hung with Kentucky; Poteet wouldn't let Nash get the ball, and early in the last half, the Heels edged ahead. Smith signaled to Brown to execute the offensive plan. Brown took the ball to the middle of the court and the other four players spread out. Brown promptly got a layup. The second time they spread out, Brown hit Shaffer for a layup. "Hey, you know, this thing works," Shaffer thought to himself. A sportswriter said legendary Kentucky Coach Adolph Rupp "didn't know whether to spit or wind his watch."

Toward the end of the game, "Nash was so frustrated he just went over and stood to the side, where he and Poteet watched the other guys go four-on-four." Carolina won 68-66.

And that "thing" without a name that was a key part of Smith's plan? It would eventually be called The Four Corners.

Successful living – like successful coaching -- takes planning. You go to school to improve your chances for a better paying job. You use blueprints to build your home. You plan for retirement. You map out your vacation to have the best time. You even plan your children -- sometimes.

Your best-laid plans, however, sometimes get wrecked by events and circumstances beyond your control. The economy goes into the tank; a debilitating illness strikes; a hurricane hits. Life is capricious and thus no plans -- not even your best ones -- are foolproof.

But you don't have to go it alone. God has plans for your life that guarantee success as God defines it if you will make him your planning partner. God's plan for your life includes joy, love, peace, kindness, gentleness, and faithfulness, all the elements necessary for truly successful living for today and for all eternity. And God's plan will not fail.

If you don't know where you are going, you will wind up somewhere else.

-- Yogi Berra

Your plans help ensure a successful life; God's plans absolutely ensure a successful eternity.

DAY 16

HOW WE LEAVE

Read 2 Kings 2:1-12.

"A chariot of fire and horses of fire appeared and separated the two of them, and Elijah went up to heaven in a whirlwind" (v. 11).

Dean Smith left exactly as he said he would.

He had said publicly that he would not announce his decision before a season began that it would be his last. "Could you imagine how many rocking chairs I'd get?" he said. "And all those people acting like they like you?" He also had no wish to saddle his successor with a team that didn't meet the standards for excellence expected of UNC. He would not quit in April either because for some time he had always felt like quitting in April and thus didn't trust those feelings.

The pattern had become virtually the same every year. "After the season we'd get him out to play golf, get him to relax," said his successor, Bill Guthridge, who in his three years at the helm won more games than any other head coach in his first two seasons (58) and became only the third coach in history to reach two Final Fours in his first three years. By late August, Guthridge said, Smith would always be sick of golf, and "we had him. This time the season rolled around, and he wasn't quite ready."

So when UNC announced a press conference for Thursday, Oct. 9, 1997, about men's basketball, those who had listened to Smith over the years knew what was about to happen. The late date meant the school would have no time to organize a search committee, so Guthridge would be offered the job and he would have to take it. With six returning regulars from the Final Four team of 1996-97, the cupboard was well stocked.

Dean Smith left the UNC basketball program exactly the way he ran it for 36 seasons: just like he wanted to.

Like Elijah and unlike Dean Smith, we can't always choose the exact circumstances under which we leave. For instance, you probably haven't always chosen the moves you've made in your life. Perhaps your company transferred you. A landlord didn't renew your lease. An elderly parent needed your care.

Sometimes the only choice we have about leaving is the manner in which we go, whether we depart with style and grace or not. Our exit from life is the same way. Unless we usurp God's authority over life and death, we can't choose how we die, just how we handle it. Perhaps the most frustrating aspect of dying is that we have at most very little control over the process. As with our birth, our death is in God's hands. We finally must surrender to his will even if we have spent a lifetime refusing to do so.

We do, however, control our destination. How we leave isn't up to us; where we spend eternity is -- and that depends on our relationship with Jesus.

This'll be really big news back home. Unless Dean Smith retires tomorrow, that is.
-- N.C. State's Jim Valvano after his Wolfpack won the 1983 NCAA championship

How you go isn't up to you; where you go is.

NORTH CAROLINA

DAY 17

DANCING ANGELS

Read Luke 15:1-10.

"There is rejoicing in the presence of the angels of God over one sinner who repents" (v. 10).

The celebration was so wild Tar Heel coach John Bunting gave up trying to find the opposing coach to shake his hand.

On Oct. 30, 2004, Carolina's football team gave its fans a Halloween treat by upsetting fourth-ranked, previously unbeaten Miami 31-28. The win came on freshman placekicker Connor Barth's last-second, 42-yard field goal. It marked the first time in history Carolina had beaten a team ranked in the top five.

A maligned Tar Heel defense stuffed the high-flying Canes, holding them to 77 yards on the ground. Third-string running back Chad Scott carried 25 times for 175 yards and two touchdowns despite an injured hip. "Chad was huge," Bunting said of Scott, forced into the game because of injuries to the backs ahead of him.

Collectively, the Carolina offensive line was another game hero, giving quarterback Darian Durant enough time to complete 21 of 29 passes for 266 yards and two touchdowns. "Our offensive line is the strength of our team," Bunting said. "We saw some things on film that made us believe we could run the ball." For the game, the Heels rolled up 545 yards of total offense.

After Barth's kick completed the upset, ecstatic Carolina fans celebrated by rushing onto the field and pulling down the goalposts. Barth joked he might well have a concussion from the many congratulatory slaps on the helmet he received.

"This win probably ranks right up there with our Florida State win [41-9 in 2001]," Bunting said. The head Tar Heel made an honest effort to find Miami coach Larry Coker for a postgame handshake, but he couldn't wend his way through the celebrating Carolina mob.

UNC just whipped Miami in football or Duke in basketball. You got that new job or that promotion. You just held your newborn child in your arms. Life has those grand moments that call for celebration. You may jump up and down and scream in a wild frenzy or share a quiet, sedate candlelight dinner at home -- but you celebrate.

Consider then a celebration that is actually beyond our imagining, one that fills every niche and corner of the very home of God and the angels. Imagine a celebration in Heaven, which also has its grand moments.

They are touched off when someone comes to faith in Jesus. Heaven itself rings with the joyous sounds of the singing and dancing of the celebrating angels. Even God rejoices when just one person – you or someone you have introduced to Christ? -- turns to him.

When you said "yes" to Christ, you made the angels dance.

When it comes to celebrating, act like you've been there before.
                                                              -- Terry Bowden

God himself joins the angels
in heavenly celebration when a single person
turns to him through faith in Jesus.

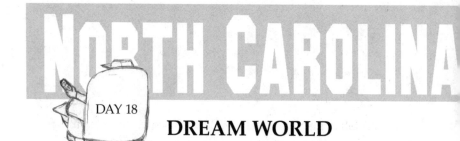
DAY 18

DREAM WORLD

Read Joel 2:26-28.

"Your old men will dream dreams, your young men will see visions" (v. 28).

Even as they sat in the ashes of their dreams, they dared to dream again.

The simple truth is that young men come to Chapel Hill to play basketball so they can win lots of games and league titles and maybe even a national title or two. Jawad Williams, Jackie Manuel, and Melvin Scott were no different when they arrived on campus in the fall of 2001.

They were young men with great dreams.

Those dreams were quickly laid to waste by the downright unbelievable 8-20 season of 2001-02, the worst season in Carolina basketball history. The 2002-03 season was better, but the sixteen losses were the second-most in school history. The squad wound up with other also-rans in the NIT and didn't even win it. The coach resigned; the proud program was in tatters.

And yet before the start of their senior season of 2004-05, Williams, Manuel, and Scott dreamed again of a championship. "What if we did it?" Williams asked. "What if we finished this year with a national championship? From 8-20 to national champions. . . . That would be a Carolina basketball story."

Six months later, the trio helped write the story's end. On April 4, the dream that had seemed to have vanished came true when

UNC whipped Illinois 75-70 for the national championship. After the nets had been cut, the trophy claimed, the hugs shared, the tears shed, and the last cheer was nothing but an echo, someone asked Williams how he, Manuel, and Scott had known they would win the title. "How else could it have ended?" he asked. "We've been the lowest and now we're the highest. We're champions."

The dream had come true.

You have dreams just as Jawad Williams, Jackie Manuel, and Melvin Scott did. Maybe to make a lot of money. Write the great American novel. Or have the fairy-tale romance. But dreams often are crushed beneath the weight of everyday living; reality, not dreams, comes to occupy your time, attention, and effort. You've come to understand that achieving your dreams requires a combination of persistence, timing, and providence.

But what if your dreams don't come true because they're not good enough? That is, they're based on the alluring but unreliable promises of the world rather than the true promises of God, which are a sure thing.

God calls us to great achievements because God's dreams for us are greater than our dreams for ourselves. Such greatness occurs, though, only when our dreams and God's will for our lives are the same. Your dreams should be worthy of your best – and worthy of God's involvement in making them come true.

Winning the championship was a dream come true.
-- Point guard Raymond Felton

Dreams based on the world's promises
are often crushed; those based on God's promises
are a sure thing.

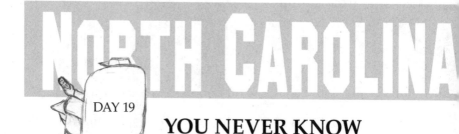
DAY 19

YOU NEVER KNOW

Read Exodus 3:1-12.

"But Moses said to God, 'Who am I, that I should go to Pharaoh and bring the Israelites out of Egypt?' And God said, 'I will be with you'" (vv. 11-12a).

He failed to make his high school team twice, didn't get any college scholarship offers, and was cut from the first college squad he tried out for. Yet he became a Carolina basketball legend.

Lennie Rosenbluth averaged 28 points a game – still the highest season average in Tar Heel history -- for UNC's 1957 team that went 32-0 and defeated Kansas and Wilt Chamberlain for the national championship. His 895 points that season remain the Carolina record as is his career scoring average of 26.9. He was All-ACC three times, and his jersey number (10) was retired.

But Rosenbluth's track record certainly didn't predict anything approaching stardom when he arrived in Chapel Hill in 1953.

He failed to make his high school team in the Bronx both as a sophomore and as a junior; he didn't even make the *junior* varsity team. He played as a senior but didn't receive a single scholarship offer. After graduation, he worked at a Catskills resort and played for the hotel's staff basketball team. By now, though, he had kept working at his game, had grown to 6'5," and could score from anywhere over anybody.

A talent scout helped arrange a tryout with North Carolina State, but the New York kid couldn't take the Carolina heat. "For me, it was hot," Rosenbluth recalled. "I'm completely out of shape and can hardly run the court without breathing heavily." He didn't get the scholarship.

That same talent scout, though, recommended Rosenbluth to Frank McGuire, who, with his unabashed fondness for New York players, gave Rosenbluth a scholarship without ever seeing him play. Even McGuire didn't know what he had on his hands.

As Lennie Rosenbluth's basketball career indicates, you just never know how things will turn out in life and what you can do. Much depends on whether – like Rosenbluth – you want it bad enough or whether – like Moses – you have to. Serving in the military, maybe even in combat. Standing by a friend while everyone else unjustly excoriates her. Undergoing agonizing medical treatment and managing to smile. You never know what life will demand of you.

It's that way too in your relationship with God. You never know where or when God will call you or what God will ask of you. You do know that God expects you to be faithful and willing to trust him even when he calls you to tasks that daunt and dismay you.

You can respond faithfully to whatever God calls you to do for him. That's because even though you never know what lies ahead, you do know that God will both lead you and provide what you need.

There's one word to describe baseball: You never know.
– Yogi Berra

**You never know what God will ask you to do,
but you always know he will provide
everything you need to do it.**

DAY 20

TEAM PLAYERS

Read 1 Corinthians 12:4-13; 27-31.

"Now to each one the manifestation of the Spirit is given for the common good" (v. 7).

What do you get when you put "a redneck, an Englishman, a Yankee and Noz" together? In North Carolina's case, you get a national championship soccer team.

Senior goalkeeper Mike Ueltschey offered the colorful description of the Carolina 2001 men's soccer team, which won the school's first soccer national title. Ueltschey – from Jackson, Miss. – was the redneck. The Englishman was fellow senior Danny Jackson. The Yankee was senior defender Chris Leitch, from Columbus, Ohio. And what was a "Noz"? That was Noz Yamauchi, a senior midfielder from Chapel Hill.

"It's funny how we all came together and became best friends," Ueltschey said. They also came together and formed the heart of a 16-4-0 team. Yamauchi led the national champions with eleven assists while the other three were the leaders of a defense that allowed less than one goal per game.

Jackson had the longest and most indirect route to Chapel Hill. Intercollegiate sports remain almost nonexistent in England, but Jackson had the notion that he could come to the States, get a college degree, and play some soccer. He wrote a few letters, and UNC coach Elmar Bolowich sent him "an eager reply."

In the College Cup – college soccer's version of the Final Four

TAR HEELS

– the Heels outlasted Stanford 3-2 in guadruple overtime in the semfinals with junior midfielder Mike Gell getting the match winner. UNC then whipped Indiana 2-0 in the finals with Jackson scoring the clinching goal on a penalty kick.

All those totally different parts from all over had come together to make a team, a national championship team in fact.

Most accomplishments are the result of teamwork, whether it's a college soccer team, the running of a household, the completion of a project at work, or a dance recital. Disparate talents and gifts work together for the common good and the greater goal.

A church works exactly the same way. At its most basic, a church is a team assembled by God. A shared faith drives the team members and impels them toward shared goals. As a successful Tar Heel soccer team must have goalkeepers, defenders, strikers, and midfielders, so must a church be composed of people with different spiritual and personal gifts. The result is something greater than everyone involved.

What makes a church team different from others is that the individual efforts are expended for the glory of God and not self. The nature of a church member's particular talents doesn't matter; what does matter is that those talents are used as part of God's team.

Money may be the most important element in modern-day stock car racing, but team chemistry runs a very close second.
— NASCAR's Bill Elliott

A church is a team of people
using their various talents and gifts for God,
the source of all those abilities to begin with.

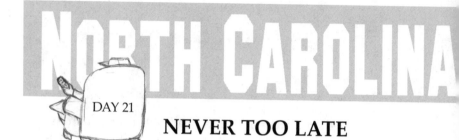
DAY 21

NEVER TOO LATE

Read Genesis 21:1-7.

"And [Sarah] added, 'Who would have said to Abraham that Sarah would nurse children? Yet I have borne him a son in his old age'" (v. 7).

Almost twenty years after he played his last game, one of North Carolina's greatest players finally got his college degree.

Larry Miller is the only two-time ACC Player of the Year in UNC history. He played from 1966-68 and still holds the school record for scoring in double figures in 64 consecutive games. He was a first-team All-America in 1968, such a great leaper he could put both elbows on the rim while dunking the ball.

Miller became one of the most important players Dean Smith ever recruited because practically every school in the country wanted him. His final choices came down to Duke and UNC. "When Miller came, that just turned the whole thing around," said Billy Cunningham, who was a senior when Miller was a freshman.

In Miller's three seasons, the Heels won two ACC tournaments; his junior season they lost to Duke by one point. In both Miller's junior and senior seasons, Carolina reached the Final Four, losing to UCLA and Lew Alcindor in the finals in 1968.

Miller went on to play in the now-defunct ABA until 1974 when he left basketball for good and went into real estate. As the years passed, he nursed an ongoing regret that he finally resolved. "I was one of the few Dean ever had who didn't graduate," Miller said. So in 1985, nearly twenty years after he had left the campus, he went back, commuting from Virginia Beach to Chapel Hill twice each week to take the one class he needed.

"They treated me just like a scholarship athlete," Miller said. "I had to report to Coach [Bill] Guthridge on my progress." He made a B-plus in the one course he needed.

Getting that college degree as Larry Miller did. Running a marathon. Getting married. Starting a new career. Though we may make all kinds of excuses, it's often never too late for life-changing decisions and milestones.

This is especially true in our faith life, which is based on God's promises. Abraham was 100 and Sarah was 90 when their first child was born. They were old folks even by the Bible's standards at the dawn of history. But God had promised them a child and just as God always does, he kept his promise no matter how unlikely it seemed.

God has made us all a promise of new life and hope through Jesus Christ. At any time in our lives – today even -- we can regret the things we have done wrong and the way we have lived, ask God in Jesus' name to forgive us for them, and discover a new way of living – forever.

It's never too late to change. God promised.

It's never too late to achieve success in sports.
         -- Brooke de Lench, writer and lecturer on children and sports

It's never too late to change a life
by turning it over to Jesus.

DAY 22

ANSWERING THE CALL

Read 1 Samuel 3:1-18.

"The Lord came and stood there, calling as at the other times, 'Samuel! Samuel!' Then Samuel said, 'Speak, for your servant is listening'" (v. 10).

The 2009 Tar Heel baseball team was loaded with stars. And then there was Garrett Gore. All he did was everything he could to help the team win.

The Heels of '09 made the school's fourth straight trip to the College World Series. The team went 48-18 and finished ranked in the top five. ACC Player-of-the-Year Dustin Ackley became the fourth Tar Heel in history to be named the National Player of the Year. The junior set several school records on his way to becoming the first three-time All-America in UNC history.

Levi Michael was a freshman All-America. Senior right-hander Adam Warren was an ESPN Academic All-America; junior pitcher Alex White led the ACC in strikeouts. Reliever Brian Moran was third-team All-America. Seven players were drafted by the pros.

Stars all over the place. Just as valuable as any of those players to the team, however, was Gore, a senior who answered the call for the sake of the team over and over again. Gore started out playing second base, took swings at third and at shortstop, and moved to rightfield his senior year. "He's an unbelievable athlete," and "the best second baseman that I've ever played with," said UNC catcher Mike McKee of his friend. Gore even willingly took a move to the bench his junior season to help the team by becoming the designated hitter for a spell.

"Garrett's been all about the team ever since he got here," Coach Mike Fox said. "He came to me about playing the outfield. To kind of say, 'Coach, I don't care where I play.'" Batting second in the lineup, Gore hit .311 and set a College World Series record when he appeared in his 21st game in Omaha.

Garrett Gore answered the call to make winners of both the Tar Heels and himself.

A team player is someone who does whatever the coach calls upon him to do for the good of the team. Something quite similar occurs when God places a specific call upon a Christian's life.

This is much scarier, though, than shifting positions on a baseball team as Garrett Gore did. The way many folks understand it is that answering God's call means going into the ministry, packing the family up, and moving halfway around the world to some place where folks have never heard of air conditioning, fried chicken, penicillin, paved roads, or the Tar Heels. Zambia. The Philippines. Cleveland even.

Not for you, no thank you. And who can blame you?

But God usually calls folks to serve him where they are. In fact, God put you where you are right now, and he has a purpose in placing you there. Wherever you are, you are called to serve him.

It's how you show up at the showdown that counts.
— Coach Homer Norton

God calls you to serve him right now
right where you are.

DAY 23

LIMITED-TIME OFFER

Read Psalm 103.

*"As for man, his days are like grass, he flourishes like a
flower of the field; the wind blows over it and it is gone.
. . . But from everlasting to everlasting the Lord's love is
with those who fear him" (vv. 15-17).*

The stage was set for the Tar Heels to return to gridiron glory
after years in the hinterlands. And then Jim Tatum died.

After "Big Jim" Tatum led Maryland to glory that included the
national championship in 1953, he shocked the sports world by
deciding to return to his beloved alma mater in 1956. The move
was a surprise because he had built Maryland into "a championship factory" while at Chapel Hill he was "starting at the
bottom of the ladder," inheriting "a team that [had] been kicked
around in recent years."

Tatum was a larger-than-life figure, and not just because he
stood 6'3" and weighed 230 pounds. He was a cockeyed optimist
whose bubbling enthusiasm was contagious, "a stalking sideline
giant who not only coached but led the cheers." Al Goldstein, an
All-American end in 1958, once said, "I hope my son can play for
a coach like [Tatum] one day."

Wade Smith, a team captain, told the story that in 1958, Tatum
declared the Heels would have a better chance against Tennessee
if it rained in Knoxville. "So he wore a raincoat to practice every
day," Smith recalled. "And do you know it rained? We won 21-7."

TAR HEELS

In 1957, Tatum's second year, UNC went 6-4, the first winning season since 1949. Another 6-4 season followed in 1958, but Smith, Goldstein, quarterback Jack Cummings and other of the best players were returning for 1959. Tatum believed his Heels would be a powerhouse.

On Wednesday, July 15, though, Tatum began feeling bad. By Friday, he was home in bed, and Saturday he went into the hospital. He died the following Thursday, July 23, 1959, of Rocky Mountain spotted fever. He was only 46.

A heart attack, cancer, some unexpected illness, or an accident will probably take -- or has already taken -- someone you know or love who is "too young to die" such as Jim Tatum.

The death of a younger person never seems to "make sense." That's because such a death belies the common view of death as the natural end of a life lived well and lived long. Moreover, you can't see the whole picture as God does, so you can't know how the death furthers God's kingdom.

At such a time, you can seize the comforting truth that God is in control and therefore everything will be all right one day. You can also gain a sense of urgency in your own life by appreciating that God's offer of life through Jesus Christ is a limited-time offer that expires at your death – and there's no guarantee about when that will be.

No one knows when he or she is going to die, so if we're going to accept Christ, we'd better not wait; death can come in the blink of an eye.
--Bobby Bowden

God offers you life through Jesus Christ, but you must accept it before your death when it expires.

DAY 24

AMAZING!

Read: Luke 4:31-36.

"All the people were amazed and said to each other, 'What is this teaching? With authority and power he gives orders to evil spirits and they come out!'" (v. 36)

One of UNC's greatest basketball players had eyesight so bad that he literally could not see the basket.

Playing from 1939-'41, George Glamack was twice the National Player of the Year and a two-time All-America. He set UNC's career scoring record with 916 points and held the top five single-game scoring records, led by the 45 points he poured in against Clemson in 1941, also a Southern Conference record

A football injury left Glamack's left eye completely blind for six months, damage from which he never fully recovered. So how in the world could he score – and score so proficiently?

"I designed a braille system all my own watching the black lines on the floor near the basket," Glamack said. "I never saw the basket, but I saw the backboard. . . . I just got to my spot on the floor and shot from there."

Glamack was 6'7", tall for that day, and he used his height to advantage by developing an unstoppable hook shoot. Plus, he had a great guard named Bob Rose. Teammate Lew Hayworth said Glamack had an "uncanny feel of the area within 15 feet of the basket. . . . Bob Rose was a tremendous ballhandler and passer for those days and he'd always be able to get the ball inside to George somehow." Glamack once acknowledged Rose as the reason he made All-America.

Glamack tried contact lenses, probably the first basketball player in the country to do so, but "I could only wear them for short periods, and then my eyes started to burn." Amazingly, the "Blind Bomber," as he became known, played better when his vision was its worst.

The word *amazing* defines the limits of what you believe to be plausible or usual. The Grand Canyon, the birth of your children, a successful basketball player who can't even see the basket -- they're amazing! You've never seen anything like that before!

Some people in Galilee felt the same way when they encountered Jesus. Jesus amazed them with the authority of his teaching, and he wowed them with his power over spirit beings. People everywhere just couldn't quit talking about him.

It would have been amazing had they not been amazed. They were, after all, witnesses to the most amazing spectacle in the history of the world: God himself was right there among them walking, talking, teaching, preaching, and healing.

Their amazement should be a part of your life too because Jesus still lives. The almighty God of the universe seeks to spend time with you every day – because he loves you. Amazing!

It's amazing. Some of the greatest characteristics of being a winning football player are the same ones it's true to be a Christian man.
-- Bobby Bowden

**Everything about God is amazing,
but perhaps most amazing of all is that he loves us
and desires our company.**

DAY 25

LIVE ACTION

Read James 2:14-26.

"Faith by itself, if it is not accompanied by action, is dead" *(v. 17).*

A Seminole did the talking first. The Heels did the playing last. The result was the greatest last-half comeback in North Carolina basketball history.

The national champions of 1993 were 16-1 and undefeated in ACC play when they hosted No. 19 FSU on Jan. 27 in the Dean Dome. The season before, FSU guard Sam Cassell had derided the Carolina fans as "a wine-and-cheese crowd" after a Seminole win. At halftime of the '93 game, Cassell was at it again, "woofing in the locker room . . . that a 'white boy,' Henrik Rodl, couldn't guard him."

For a while, Cassell had room to talk as for almost 30 minutes the Seminoles dominated the game, leading 69-49 with 10:23 left. But Rodl nailed a three-pointer to start a remarkable run that drove the Dome crowd to its frenzied feet and left it there for the duration of the game. "The 3-pointers began to fall, the UNC steals began to pile up, and sophomore guard Donald Williams began to catch fire."

The Heels scored fifteen straight points over 2:10. When Derrick Phelps hit two free throws with 3:15 left, FSU led by a single point, and the Dome was a madhouse. After the teams traded baskets, senior forward George Lynch – whom the national champions would vote as the team MVP – completely brought the house down. He stole a pass and slammed the dunk home to propel the Heels into the lead with 1:41 to play. The steal coincidentally put Lynch at No. 1 on the school's all-time list.

The rest seemed almost anti-climactic. FSU missed on its next two possessions, and Williams hit four straight free throws. UNC won 82-77, and the Heel fans poured into the court to celebrate.

FSU's Cassell was left with only one thing to say, and to his credit, he said it: "They're not a wine-and-cheese crowd anymore."

Talk is cheap; after all, it doesn't cost anything. Consider your neighbor or coworker who talks without saying anything, who makes promise she doesn't keep, who brags about his own exploits, who can always tell you how to do something but never shows up for the work. As the Seminoles learned in that remarkable 1993 game, you know that words without action just don't cut it.

That principle applies in the life of a person of faith too. Merely declaring our faith isn't enough, however sincere we may be. Only when we back up our words by putting our faith into action do we shout to the world of the depth of our commitment to Christ.

Sure, Jesus preached and taught. His ministry, though, was a virtual whirlwind of activity that often left followers scrambling and panting to keep up with him. So are we today to change our world by doing, not just talking about it.

Don't talk too much or too soon.

-- Bear Bryant

Faith that does not reveal itself in action is dead.

DAY 26

BAD IDEA

Read Mark 14:43-50.

*"The betrayer had arranged a signal with them: 'The one
I kiss is the man; arrest him and lead him away under
guard'" (v. 44).*

The Board of Trustees of the University of North Carolina once
had an idea so bad that if they pulled it off today they would
stand a good chance of being tarred and feathered while they
were being run out of the state. They abolished football.

UNC played two games in its inaugural football season of 1888
and four more in 1889, all six of the games against Wake Forest
and Trinity (Duke). The records were 0-2 and 2-2 respectively
with the first-ever UNC win a 33-0 trouncing of Wake Forest in
the '89 season opener. In the second game of that second season,
team captain Steve Bragaw suffered a broken leg. Later on, player
George Graham broke his collarbone.

The trustees had seen enough. They decided that "football
was far too savage a game for 'civilized' college life" and voted
to outlaw the sport. The decision plunged the school into what
was called "the Great Depression of athletics at Chapel Hill."
In a review of athletics on campus in 1890, *University Magazine*
moaned, "Little interest is shown in tennis. Baseball is dead.
Football – deader."

Football at UNC had a savior, though, in Professor Horace
Williams, who led the charge to have football reinstated. Two

other profs, F.P. Venable and Eben Alexander, and a "large group of dogmatic students" joined him and convinced the trustees to reverse their decision in time for the 1891 season. The game was placed under the supervision of the newly created University Athletic Advisory Committee with Prof. Williams as its chairman.

Reflecting that original bad idea, though, the official UNC football records skip from 1889 to 1891.

That sure-fire investment you made from a pal's hot stock tip. The expensive exercise machine that now traps dust bunnies under your bed. Blond hair. Telling your wife you wanted to eat at the restaurant with the waitresses in little shorts. They seemed like pretty good ideas at the time; they weren't.

As did the UNC Board of Trustees in 1890, we all have some bad ideas in our lifetime. They provide some of our most crucial learning experiences. Some ideas, though, are so irreparably and inherently bad that we cannot help but wonder why they were even conceived in the first place.

Almost two thousand years ago a man had just such an idea. Judas' betrayal of Jesus remains to this day one of the most heinous acts of treachery in history. Turning his back on Jesus was a bad idea for Judas then; it's a bad idea for us now.

As it stands now, our boys have no incentive to advance athletics.
– University Magazine *after the decision to outlaw football at UNC*

**We all have some pretty bad ideas
during our lifetimes, but nothing equals
the folly of turning away from Jesus.**

DAY 27

GOAL ORIENTED

Read 1 Peter 1:3-9.

"For you are receiving the goal of your faith, the salvation of your souls" (v. 9).

They didn't have any great goals." That was the situation at UNC when Dean Smith was elevated from assistant to head basketball coach on Aug. 5, 1961, according to former UNC Sports Information Director Rick Brewer.

Smith inherited a program that for all its winning ways – a national championship in 1957 and seasons of 19-7, 20-5, 18-6, and 19-4 from 1958-61 – was basically without direction. A number of factors played into creating that less than favorable situation.

For years, Coach Frank McGuire had battled with school administrators about the program's lack of money. His team didn't even have its own gymnasium, having to practice at night or share facilities with PE classes and intramural teams. McGuire felt his national champions deserved "a magnificent basketball palace," but administrators had no such plan.

A series of incidents during the 1960-61 season finished McGuire off. He often declared, "This has been the worst year of my life." Chief among the problems was the implication of two players in a nationwide points-shaving scandal, which "proved to be a knockout punch" for McGuire. When the NCAA put the basketball program on probation, an embarrassed administration responded by limiting recruiting and schedules and cutting the budget "to the barest minimum." McGuire resigned.

Into that turbid atmosphere came Dean Smith with basically one mandate: "Don't cheat." As Brewer recalled it, "The impression was the administration here didn't care about having a great winning basketball tradition anymore. They just wanted to have a basketball program, period."

Basically, they had no goals for the program; they wanted first of all to avoid any more trouble.

What are your goals for your life? Have you ever thought them out? Or do you just shuffle along living for your paycheck, staying out of trouble, and seeking whatever momentary fun you can find instead of pursuing some greater purpose?

Now try this one: What is the goal of your faith life? You go to church to worship God. You read the Bible and study God's word to learn about God and how God wants you to live. But what is it you hope to achieve? What is all that stuff about? For what purpose do you believe that Jesus Christ is God's son?

The answer is actually quite simple: The goal of your faith life is your salvation, and this is the only goal in life that matters. Nothing you will ever seek is as important or as eternal as getting into Heaven and making sure that everybody you know and love will be there too one day.

I always wanted to be a coach.

-- Dean Smith

**The most important goal of your life
is to get to Heaven and ensure that one day
you'll meet everyone you know there.**

DAY 28

BEYOND THE GAMES

Read Galatians 5:16-26.

"So I say, live by the Spirit.... The sinful nature desires what is contrary to the Spirit.... The acts of the sinful nature are obvious: ... I warn you, as I did before, that those who live like this will not inherit the kingdom of God" (vv. 16, 17, 19, 21).

The bare statistics say Phillip Deas was not a success at UNC; the reality shouts otherwise.

Deas came to Chapel Hill in 1997 as one of the most heralded high-school quarterbacks in the country. He was redshirted his freshman season and then transferred before the 1998 season started when he saw he was behind the other quarterbacks.

Nevertheless, no one had more impact on the lives of UNC's football players than Deas did while he was on the team. "He's done as much positive for this football team off the field as any player I've ever been around," Coach Carl Torbush said.

Deas was the squad's spiritual leader. In the fall of '97, he announced he was holding a Bible study in his dorm room for the team. Nobody showed up. By the spring, though, the Bible study group had grown to about sixty. Deas' "magnetic, evangelical style had won over so many teammates it was hard to keep track of the converts." In the defensive secondary alone, Quinton Savage, Antwon Black, Steve Fisher, and Jomo Legins all confessed Christ as their Savior. Black showed up for 1998's preseason practice sporting a new tattoo: a pair of praying hands.

Deas' decision to transfer was a difficult one. His announcement after a morning practice session in August left many of his teammates stunned. "He meant a lot of things to a lot of people," Savage said.

So Phillip Deas' name is nowhere in the Carolina record books. His impact, though, is written larger in the hearts and lives of those he touched. "His purpose here, it may not have been football, but it was on a higher plane, spiritual," Savage said.

Are you a successful person? Your answer, of course, depends upon how you define success. Is the measure of your success based on the number of digits in your bank balance, the square footage of your house, or that title on your office door?

Certainly the world determines success by wealth, fame, prestige, awards, and possessions. Our culture screams that life is all about gratifying your own needs and wants. If it feels good, do it. It's basically the Beach Boys' philosophy of life.

But all success of this type has one glaring shortcoming: You can't take it with you. Eventually, Daddy takes the T-bird away. Like life itself, all these things are fleeting.

A more lasting way to approach success is the way Phillip Deas does: through the spiritual rather than the physical. The goal becomes not money or backslaps by sycophants but eternal life spent with God. Success of that kind is forever.

Success demands singleness of purpose.

-- Vince Lombardi

**Success isn't permanent, and failure isn't fatal --
except in your relationship with God.**

THE PIONEER SPIRIT

Read Luke 5:1-11.

"So they pulled their boats up on shore, left everything and followed him" (v. 11).

One timeless Tar Heel play forever changed college basketball.

Art Chansky wrote that the "cable network ESPN2 . . . was created with Duke-Carolina basketball in mind." Launched in 1993, the network used the first Carolina-Duke game of each season as the hook to sell subscriptions. In the 1950s, though, televised basketball was nonexistent. A pioneer changed that.

C.D. Chesley played freshman football at UNC before transferring to Penn. In 1956, he paid the ACC $75,000 to produce three football telecasts. The following March he attended the ACC Tournament in Raleigh. In a classic semifinal game, Frank McGuire's undefeated Heels nipped Wake Forest on a famous three-point play by All-American Lennie Rosenbluth. He collided with a Wake player but got the call, the basket, and the free throw for the 61-59 Carolina win.

"Chesley got the bug. Caught up in the magic of McGuire's Miracle," Chesley set up a five-station network to televise UNC's Final Four games. Carolina won both games in triple overtime "to capture the national championship and the collective heart of a state." As Chesley recalled it, "They were renting TV sets for hospitals. . . . I knew right there that ACC basketball could be as popular as anything shown on TV in North Carolina."

TAR HEELS

The marriage of college basketball and television soon took place. In 1958, Chesley "created the first college conference TV basketball package in the country." Voted as the third most influential person in the history of the ACC behind only Everett Case and Dean Smith, the pioneering Chesley "drove his Ford station wagon from Maryland to South Carolina" to line up twenty stations that first season.

Going to a place in your life you've never been before – as C.D. Chesley did -- requires a willingness to take risks and face uncertainty head-on. You may have never changed the face of television sports broadcasting, but you've had your moments when your latent pioneer spirit manifested itself. That time you changed careers, ran a marathon, volunteered at a homeless shelter, learned Spanish, or went back to school.

While attempting new things invariably begets apprehension, the truth is that when life becomes too comfortable and too familiar, it gets boring. The same is true of God, who is downright dangerous because he calls us to be anything but comfortable as we serve him. He summons us to continuously blaze new trails in our faith life, to follow him no matter what. Stepping out on faith is risky all right, but the reward is a life of accomplishment, adventure, and joy that cannot be equaled anywhere else.

Life is an adventure. I wouldn't want to know what's going to happen next.
-- Bobby Bowden

Unsafe and downright dangerous, God calls us
out of the place where we are comfortable to a life
of adventure and trailblazing in his name.

DAY 30

PROMISES, PROMISES

Read 2 Corinthians 1:16-20.

"No matter how many promises God has made, they are 'Yes' in Christ" (v. 20).

Because a promise was kept, UNC's first football All-America once earned himself a brand new blue flannel suit for scoring a touchdown.

Coach Carl Snavely's first team went 7-1-1 in 1934, losing only to a powerful Tennessee squad 19-7 and tying N.C. State. The unquestioned star of the team was George Barclay, an All-American guard on offense and a star linebacker on defense. "George was so good, one group picked [him] at tackle," said Charlie Shaffer, who played wingback and tailback on that 1934 squad. While Shaffer called the signals at the line of scrimmage, Barclay actually called the plays in the huddle. "He was the greatest diagnostician of plays I've ever seen," Shaffer said.

In 1933 against Virginia, Barclay intercepted a pass and returned it 35 yards for a touchdown. Prior to the 1934 Cavalier game, a friend promised him "a fine suit of clothing" if he repeated his feat. Sure enough, Barclay got another pick and went 55 yards for the score. He later explained, "I anticipated a pass on the play, moved back and out from my linebacker's position, and sure enough, they threw a pass, hitting me in my mid-section, and I ran for the touchdown."

A newspaper article the next day waxed rhapsodic about

Barclay's "beautiful run for a touchdown" and how he "dodged, sidestepped, and set up [his] blockers" to score. Barclay could only laugh: "All I had to do was run straight down the field because no one was in front of me."

With every step toward the goal line, his mind was on the stylish clothes he had been promised. Sure enough, two weeks later he had his spiffy new suit.

The promises you make don't say much about you; the promises you keep tell everything.

The promise to your daughter to be there for her softball game. To your son to help him with his math homework. To your parents to come see them soon. To your spouse to remain faithful until death parts you. And remember what you promised God?

You may carelessly throw promises around, but you can never outpromise God, who is downright profligate with his promises. For instance, he has promised to love you always, to forgive you no matter what you do, and to prepare a place for you with him in Heaven.

And there's more good news in that God operates on this simple premise: Promises made are promises kept. You can rely absolutely on God's promises. The people to whom you make them should be able to rely just as surely on your promises.

In the everyday pressures of life, I have learned that God's promises are true.

-- Major leaguer Garret Anderson

**God keeps his promises just as those
who rely on you expect you to keep yours.**

THE HEALING TOUCH

Read Matthew 17:14-20.

"If you have faith as small as a mustard seed, you can say to this mountain, 'Move from here to there' and it will move. Nothing will be impossible for you" (v. 20).

By all accounts, Mike Pepper should have died. When he didn't, he knew who had a hand in it.

In the spring of 1977, Pepper was impressed by his recruiting trip to Chapel Hill. "I was hanging out on my visit with all these guys I'd seen on TV all year. It was unbelievable," he said. Assistant coach Bill Guthridge delivered the bad news, though, that while the Heels were interested in Pepper, they didn't have a scholarship available for him. Only after Pepper's visit did a scholarship for a point guard open up; he got it.

He was a key reserve his junior year and then a starter and a co-captain in 1980-81 on the team Al Wood led to the national finals. The highlight of his career came in the ACC Tournament semifinals against Wake Forest. He hit a 20-foot jumper with eight seconds to play for a 58-57 Carolina win.

More than 20 years later, Pepper was still playing basketball in pickup games. As he shot a free throw in December 2003, though, something went wrong. "I had this very uneasy, awkward feeling," he recalled. What he had was a life-threatening aneurysm that was leaking blood and probably should have already killed him.

Pepper underwent immediate brain surgery and lapsed into

a coma. "Most people in his situation would have died," said his doctor. Even if Pepper survived, severe brain damage was a real possibility. Not only did he make it, but he recovered completely, even playing basketball again.

Pepper understood the part the doctors played in his recovery, but he knew someone else was involved. "I'm so thankful the good Lord looked after me," he said.

Mike Pepper's healing was miraculous. If we believe in healing that occurs outside the usual strictures of medical care, we have pretty much come to consider it to be a relatively rare occurrence. All too often, our initial reaction when we are ill or hurting is to call a doctor rather than to pray. If we really want to move a mountain, we'll round up some heavy-duty earthmoving equipment.

The truth is, though, that divine healing occurs with quite astonishing regularity; the problem is our perspective. We are usually quite effusive in our thanks to and praise for a doctor or a particular medicine without considering that God is the one responsible for all healing.

We should remember also that "natural" healing occurs because our bodies react as God created them to. Those healings, too, are divine; they, too, are miraculous. Faith healing is really nothing more – or less – than giving credit where credit is due.

To come back on the ice was hard, and at the same time it was kind of a healing process.
-- Olympic champion Ekaterina Gordeeva

God does in fact heal continuously everywhere;
all too often we just don't notice.

DAY 32

FATHER FIGURE

Read Matthew 3:13-17.

"A voice from heaven said, 'This is my Son, whom I love; with him I am well pleased'" (v. 17).

Ty Lawson grumbled and fussed, but in the end he could only thank his father for all his dad had put him through.

Lawson was the point guard for the 2009 Carolina national champions and the ACC Player of the Year. He won the Bob Cousy Award in 2009 as the nation's best collegiate point guard and was the 18th player taken in the NBA draft.

On that national championship night in Detroit, watching proudly was Ty's father, George, who had shared a dream with his son since Ty was five and George started drilling him in basketball. George would position himself at the foul line, place Ty at the baseline, and then have his son dribble at him full speed, executing dribbling moves George barked at him. George called those exercises "commandos," and he coupled them with shooting sessions in which Ty's penalty for missing shots was more commandos.

When Ty was 12, his father would drive them to a hill and the two would run up and down together. "It was crazy steep, and long too," Ty recalled. "My whole body would hurt after that." But that drill, he said, helped develop the blinding speed on the court that was his trademark.

Commandos, hill running, 6 a.m. shooting sessions, physical

pickup games against servicemen 20 years older than he – Ty did them all, grumbling often but yielding always to his dad's commands. "Dad pushed me to play basketball," Ty said, "but I'm thankful for it." Ty's mother, Jackie, liked the basketball life. "That was what I considered quality father-son time," she said.

And that quality father-son time led Ty all the way to a national championship and the NBA.

American society largely belittles and marginalizes fathers and their influence upon their sons. Men are necessary to effect pregnancy; after that, they can leave and everybody's better off.

But we need look in only two places to appreciate the enormity of that misconception: our jails – packed with males who lacked the influence of fathers in their lives as they grew up -- and the Bible. God – being God – could have chosen any relationship he desired between Jesus and himself, including society's approach of irrelevancy. Instead, the most important relationship in all of history was that of father-son. God obviously believes a close, loving relationship between fathers and sons, such as that of George and Ty Lawson, is crucial. For men and women to espouse otherwise or for men to walk blithely and carelessly out of their children's lives constitutes disobedience to the divine will.

Simply put, God loves fathers. After all, he is one.

My dad was a huge influence on me. I imagine if he had put a wrench in my hand I would have been a great mechanic.
-- Pete Maravich

**Fatherhood is a tough job, but a model
for the father-child relationship is found
in that of Jesus the Son with God the Father.**

DAY 33

NAME DROPPING

Read Exodus 3:13-20.

*"God said to Moses, 'I AM WHO I AM. This is what
you are to say to the Israelites: 'I AM has sent me to you'"
(v. 14).*

From "Choo Choo" to the "B.V.D. Boys," nicknames have been a
part of UNC's long sports history from the very beginning.

So named because of the speed they displayed on the court,
the "White Phantoms" of 1924 went 26-0 and won UNC's first
basketball national championship. Perhaps the most startling
Carolina nickname belongs to Nat "Bloody Neck" Cartmell,
UNC's first basketball coach. The origins of his startling moniker
have been lost, though it may come from a childhood accident in
which he cut two and a half fingers off his right hand.

The most renowned nickname in Carolina sports history is
that of the legendary Charlie "Choo Choo" Justice, who received
his appellation because it was said he "ran like a choo-choo
train on a snaking, uneven track." The "B.V.D. Boys" of 1967-68
earned their nickname when they showed up for a tournament
in Portland and their practice gear didn't. Coach Dean Smith
cleared the arena of spectators, and the players practiced in their
underwear. Fully clothed, they won the tournament.

Guard George Barclay was labeled "King George the First,"
because in 1934 he was UNC's first football All-America. The
powerhouse 1929 football team is still known as "The Team of a

TAR HEELS

Million Backs." The squad actually had seventeen backs, which was enough to romp to a 9-1 record and score 346 points.

UNC's use of "Tar Heel" obviously comes from North Carolina's being The Tar Heel State, but those origins are shrouded in history. One legend derives from a letter about a Civil-War battle involving men from North Carolina. Gen. Robert E. Lee said of them, "They stand as if they have tar on their heels."

Nicknames are not slapped haphazardly upon individuals but rather reflect widely held perceptions about the person named. Proper names do that also.

Nowhere throughout history has this concept been more prevalent that in the Bible, where a name is not a mere label but is an expression of the essential nature of the named one. That is, a person's name reveals his or her character. Even God shares this concept; to know the name of God is to know God as he has chosen to reveal himself to us.

What does your name say about you? Honest, trustworthy, a seeker of the truth and a person of God? Or does the mention of your name cause your coworkers to whisper snide remarks, your neighbors to roll their eyes, or your friends to start making allowances for you? Most importantly, what does your name say about you to God? He, too, knows you by name.

A good nickname inspires awe and ensures that you'll be enshrined in the Pantheon of [Sports] Legends.
-- Funny Sports Quotes blog

**Live so that your name evokes
positive associations by people you know,
by the public, and by God.**

DAY 34

THE ANSWER

Read Colossians 2:2-10.

*"My purpose is that they . . . may know the mystery of
God, namely, Christ, in whom are hidden all the treasures
of wisdom and knowledge" (vv. 2, 3).*

Steve Fisher's life at UNC was going nowhere – and then he
found the answer.

He walked on to the Carolina football team in 1995 and saw
little action his freshman and sophomore seasons. In his junior
season, he "developed into maybe the best special-teams player
on the squad" but still had no scholarship. As the season wound
down, he considered transferring. With All-ACC cornerback
Robert Williams ahead of him, he wouldn't play much his senior
year. "I was seriously thinking about moving on out," he said.

His life off the football field wasn't any better either. "I was
partying all the time," Fisher recalled. "My grades were bad. . . . If
you follow the crowd, it'll take over your life. That was what was
happening to me."

One morning his uncle, a minister, called and talked him into
spending some time with family. While he was home, Fisher
admitted that his life was in real trouble. His uncle suggested an
answer. "That day, I decided to give Jesus Christ a chance," Fisher
said. "Everything started changing right after that."

Did it ever. "He's turned his life around," said quarterback
Oscar Davenport. Fisher's grades went up; teammates noticed the

change and began to regard him as a team leader. He became the Tar Heels' Bible study leader.

After the 1997 Gator Bowl, Williams turned pro, Coach Mack Brown left for Texas, and new coach Carl Torbush awarded Fisher a scholarship. When the 1998 season started, so did Fisher.

"The Lord took care of things for me," Fisher said. He found his answer in Jesus.

Experience is essentially the uncovering of answers to some of life's questions, both trivial and profound. You often discover to your dismay that as soon as you learn a few answers, the questions change. Your children get older, your health worsens, your financial situation changes -- all situations requiring answers to a new set of difficulties.

No answers, though, are more important than those you seek in your search for God and the meaning of life because they determine your fate for all eternity. Since a life of faith is a journey and not a destination, the questions do indeed change with your circumstances. The "why" or the "what" you ask God when you're a teenager is vastly different from the quandaries you ponder as an adult.

No matter how you phrase the question, though, the answer inevitably centers on Jesus. And that answer never changes.

When you're a driver and you're struggling in the car, you're looking for God to come out of the sky and give you a magical answer.
-- NASCAR's Rusty Wallace

**It doesn't matter what the question is;
if it has to do with life, temporal or eternal,
the answer lies in Jesus.**

DAY 35

PRECIOUS MEMORIES

Read 1 Thessalonians 3:6-13.

"Timothy . . . has brought good news about your faith and love. He has told us that you always have pleasant memories of us" (v. 6).

Antawn Jamison remembered.

Jamison was one of Carolina's greatest basketball players, the first UNC player in history to be chosen first-team All-ACC as a freshman (1996). He was All-ACC three times before turning pro after the 1997-98 season.

That season Jamison scored 822 points, the third highest single-season total in school history. He was All-America and the National Player of the Year. He left Chapel Hill eighth in career points and second in career rebounds. Today, he is third in career caroms, only ten off Tyler Hansbrough's record of 409.

Jamison came to North Carolina courtesy of Hurricane Hugo. His father was a carpenter who moved his family from Louisiana to get a construction job. Antawn was 12 at the time, and he admitted, "If the hurricane hadn't come through, I probably wouldn't be in a Carolina uniform."

Jamison's parents were young when he was born. His father's job required him to travel, and his mother put in long shifts as a cashier. Much of the parenting duties when Jamison was a young child fell to his paternal grandmother, Annie Lee Jamison.

She died when he was a junior in high school, but Jamison

always remembered her when he played basketball. At Carolina, in the locker room before each game, he said a prayer while clutching a ring that belonged to her. Then before he took the floor for the first time at each game, he pointed to the arena roof, a personal reminder of the woman he called Mama.

Antawn Jamison didn't forget.

As is the case with Antawn Jamison's beloved grandmother, your whole life will one day be only a memory because – hold your breath for this red-hot news flash -- you will die. With that knowledge in hand, you can get busy and make some preparations for that fateful day such as selecting a funeral home, purchasing a cemetery plot and picking out your casket or opting for cremation, and designating the one who will deliver your eulogy.

What you cannot control about your death, however, is how you will be remembered and whether your demise leaves a gaping hole in the lives of those with whom you shared your life or a pothole that's quickly paved over. What determines whether the tears that fall at your death result from heartfelt grief or a sinus infection?

Love does. Just as Paul wrote, the love you give away during your life decides whether or not memories of you will be precious and pleasant.

I don't want my children to remember me as a professional football player. I want them to remember me as a man of God.
– Reggie White

How you will be remembered after you die
is largely determined by how much
and how deeply you love others now.

DAY 36

SMART MOVE

Read 1 Kings 4:29-34; 11:1-6.

"[Solomon] was wiser than any other man. . . . As Solomon grew old, his wives turned his heart after other gods, and his heart was not fully devoted to the Lord his God" (vv. 4:31, 11:4).

As the opening game of what would be the national championship season of 1981-82 neared, Dean Smith had yet to name his team's fifth starter. Only two days before the opener, he decided on a freshman named Jordan.

This was the season of "The Shot," "the most famous play in Tar Heel history and one of the most famous in college athletics." Michael Jordan's 16-foot shot from the left wing with only fifteen seconds left propelled the Heels to a 63-62 win over Georgetown and Smith's first national championship. The shot also "launched Michael Jordan as the greatest player in the sport's history."

With Kansas looming on Nov. 28, 1981, though, neither Jordan nor Smith knew for sure who would be starting. James Worthy, Sam Perkins, Matt Doherty, and Jimmy Black were locks, but that fifth spot was still open. The competition was between Jordan and junior Jimmy Braddock. "We figured it would be Michael," Black said because Black was the starting point guard and Braddock was more of a point guard than Jordan was.

Smith explained that he made his decision because "while Braddock was a good defender, Michael was a little quicker and

TAR HEELS

at least four inches taller." Jordan joined Phil Ford, James Worthy, and Mike O'Loren as the only freshmen Smith had ever started in season openers.

The top-ranked Tar Heels won 74-67 with Jordan making a modest debut by scoring 12 points. As Braddock put it, "You could already see we'd be a better team with [Jordan] starting."

Smith's belated decision ultimately turned out to be one really smart move.

Remember that time you wrecked the car when you spilled hot coffee on your lap? That cold morning you fell out of the boat? The time you gave your honey a tool box for her birthday?

Formal education notwithstanding, we all make some dumb moves sometime because time spent in a classroom is not an accurate gauge of common sense. Folks impressed with their own smarts often grace us with erudite pronouncements that we intuitively recognize as flawed, unworkable, or simply wrong.

A good example is the observation that great intelligence and scholarship are not compatible with faith in God. That is, the more we know, the less we believe. But any incompatibility occurs only because we begin to trust in our own wisdom rather than the wisdom of God. We forget, as Solomon did, that God is the ultimate source of all our knowledge and wisdom and that even our ability to learn is a gift from God.

Not smart at all.

Michael really won the job with his defense.
-- Dean Smith, explaining his decision to start Jordan

Being truly smart means trusting in God's wisdom rather than only in our own knowledge.

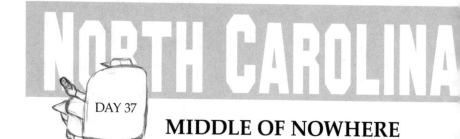
DAY 37

MIDDLE OF NOWHERE

Read Genesis 28:10-22.

"When Jacob awoke from his sleep, he thought, 'Surely the Lord is in this place, and I was not aware of it'" (v. 16).

You have to look real hard on the map to find it. Right there in the middle of nowhere, UNC found its greatest women's basketball player ever.

When she finished her remarkable career as a Tar Heel in 2007, point guard Ivory Latta left behind a four-year record of 121-17 that included three ACC championships, two Final Fours, and an Elite Eight. She was a two-time All-America, ESPN's National Player of the Year in 2006, and the 2006 ACC Player of the Year. She is UNC's all-time leading scorer and is the only player, male or female, to be named ACC Tournament MVP three times.

"Ivy" -- as the homefolks call her -- grew up in McConnells, S.C., pop. 200. One block building houses McConnells' two-room town hall, its post office, and its fire department. The town once had a railroad station, a big general store, a cotton gin, and a peach shed. But "the cotton gin burned, the peach orchards played out, and the railroad line was pulled up. . . . Even the general store was torn down." Now McConnells' entire business district consists of two convenience stores that glare at each other from opposite sides of the highway.

It's mostly farm country with some beef and dairy cattle that hasn't changed much since a 1780 Revolutionary War battle was fought at a nearby site called Brattonsville where Mel Gibson filmed some scenes from *The Patriot*.

Not surprisingly, Latta didn't have much to do except play sports when she was growing up there in the middle of nowhere. Tar Heel fans should forever be grateful, though, for that bucolic little place just over from Bullock Creek.

Ever been to Bear Grass? What about Toluca? Or Old Deck, which is just up the road from Ash and not too far from Nakin, Bug Hill, and Dulah?

They are among the many small communities, some of them nothing more than crossroads, that dot the North Carolina countryside. Not on any interstate highway or even a four-lane highway, they seem to be in the middle of nowhere, the type of place where Ivory Latta could be found as a child dribbling a basketball. They're just hamlets we zip through on our way to somewhere important.

But don't be misled; those villages are indeed special and wonderful. That's because God is in Pinetops and Cofield just as he is in Charlotte, Rocky Mount, and Chapel Hill. Even when you are far off the roads well traveled, you are with God. As Jacob discovered one rather astounding morning, the middle of nowhere is, in fact, holy ground -- because God is there.

The middle of nowhere is the place that teaches you that crossing the goal line first is not as important as the course you took to get there.
— Dive instructor Ridlon Kiphart

**No matter how far off the beaten path you travel,
you are still on holy ground because God is there.**

DAY 38

THE NIGHTMARE

Read Mark 1:21-27.

"Have you come to destroy us? I know who you are – the Holy one of God!" (v. 24)

The night before the Duke game of 1970, Tar Heel running back Don McCauley had nightmares.

Coach Bill Dooley called McCauley "the greatest football player I've ever seen." As a senior in 1970, he set an NCAA record with 1,720 yards rushing. He set 23 school records during his All-American career, many of which still stand (including his 21 touchdowns and 2,021 all-purpose yards in 1970). He was twice the ACC Player of the Year.

McCauley paced Dooley's Heels to an 8-3 record in 1970, but despite all his success, recurring nightmares kept him awake the eve of the season's last game. "I had trouble sleeping," he said. "I was scared to death, thinking about this being my last game at home and everything. . . . I wasn't even thinking about records." Perhaps contributing to his anxiety was a write-up he had read that day saying Duke would not let him break away.

So what happened? He rushed for 279 yards and scored five touchdowns (both school records at the time) as the Heels simply blasted Duke 59-34. McCauley also set a school record (tied by Mike Voight against Duke in 1976) by carrying the ball 47 times, thirteen more carries than the entire Duke team had.

Ken Rappaport wrote, "Not even Choo Choo Justice in his

finest hour ever received the thunderous ovation that McCauley did. . . . For the last several minutes the 48,000 fans chanted, 'We want McCauley. We want McCauley.'" Three times in an effort to get to their hero, fans rushed onto the field before the game was over and had to be pushed back. When the game ended, they swept McCauley up and carried him across the field.

In the end, the Blue Devils wound up living a nightmare.

Falling. Drowning. Standing naked in a crowded room. They're nightmares, dreams that jolt us from our sleep in anxiety or downright terror. The film industry has used our common nightmares to create horror movies that allow us to experience our fears vicariously. This includes the formulaic "evil vs. good" movies in which demons and the like render good virtually helpless in the face of their power and ruthlessness.

The spiritual truth, though, is that it is evil that has come face to face with its worst nightmare: Jesus. We seem to understand that our basic mission as Jesus' followers is to further his kingdom and change the world through emulating him in the way we live and love others. But do we appreciate that in truly living for Jesus, we are daily tormenting the very devil himself?

Satan and his lackeys quake in fear before the power of almighty God that is in us through Jesus.

I can't have a nightmare tonight. I've just lived through one.
-- Darrell Imhoff, the opposing center the night Wilt Chamberlain
scored 100 points.

**As the followers of Jesus Christ,
we are the stuff of Satan's nightmares.**

DAY 39

20/20 VISION

Read Acts 26:1, 9-23.

"So then, . . . I was not disobedient to the vision from heaven" (v. 19).

The Tar Heel players saw the future every time they opened their lockers. As a result, they refused to cut down some nets.

In November 1992, Coach Dean Smith and his staff gave each of the team members a photograph of the Louisiana Superdome, site of the Final Four. Written on the photos were the words "North Carolina – 1993 NCAA Champions." That carefully prepared vision had its effect on the way the players thought. "Maybe it's mental conditioning to get here," said two-time All-American center Eric Montross. "We sure had it [the national championship] in our minds."

The vision also affected the way the players behaved. For example, they refused to cut down any nets but those in New Orleans. On Dec. 5, 1992, the Heels crushed Texas 104-68 to win the Diet Pepsi Tournament of Champions, and the coliseum workers efficiently and dutifully brought out an orange ladder and a pair of scissors for the obligatory net cutting. The UNC players accepted the tournament trophy and left the court, leaving the ladder lonely and unused. The nets survived for another day.

On March 28, 1993, the Heels fought off Cincinnati 75-68 in overtime to win the NCAA Tournament's East Regional. Cue the ladder and the scissors. The players talked it over this time, gave

TAR HEELS

the nets a glance, and again decided to wait. After all, they had seen the vision. "If we want to cut down the nets, it'll be in New Orleans," said senior forward George Lynch.

And so it was. On April 5, 1993, the players finally made use of the ladder and the scissors. The nets came down after the 77-71 win over Michigan for the national championship. The vision was reality.

To speak of visions is often to risk their being lumped with palm readings, Ouija boards, seances, horoscopes, and other such useless mumbo-jumbo. The danger such mild amusements pose, however, is very real in that they indicate a reliance on something other than God. It is God who knows the future; it is God who has a vision and a plan for your life; it is God who has the answers you seek as you struggle to find your way.

You probably do have a vision for your life, a plan for how it should unfold. It's the dream you pursue through your family, your job, your hobbies, your interests.

But your vision inspires a fruitful life only if it is compatible with God's plan. As the apostle Paul found out, you ignore God's vision at your peril. If you pursue it, however, you'll find an even more glorious life than you could ever have envisioned for yourself.

They saw the future, pure and simple. It was already written down.
-- Sportswriter Warren Hynes on the 1992-93 national champions

Your grandest vision for the future
pales beside the vision God has
of what the two of you can accomplish together.

DAY 40

JUST PERFECT

Read Matthew 5:43-48.

"Be perfect, therefore, as your heavenly Father is perfect"
(v. 48).

UNC's legendary team of 1957 isn't the only squad in Tar Heel history to go undefeated and win the national championship.

In 1924, a bunch nicknamed the "White Phantoms" completed a 26-0 season with a sweep of the Southern Conference Tournament. The team was later recognized as the national champion. The perfect season was part of the first golden age of UNC basketball. The Heels won the Southern Conference championship in 1922, '24, '25, and '26. The record from 1922-26 was 93-14.

The 1924 team acquired its unique moniker during the conference tournament when a sportswriter sought a phrase to describe the effortless, almost ghost-like moves of the players. They were so fast they seemed like phantoms and so good that some writers accused them of showboating. Their coach, Norman Shepard, disagreed, declaring his players' graceful ease often made the opponents look awkward.

Monk McDonald, one of the phantoms, earned twelve letters at UNC in football, basketball, and baseball. He captained the 15-1 1923 squad and then coached the 18-5 1925 team as a first-year medical student. The star of the perfect champions was Cart Carmichael, UNC's first All-America in any sport. Jack "Sprat" Cobb, tall for the day at 6'2", matured into the National Player of the Year in 1926. He averaged 15 points a game from 1924 to 1926 in an age when three field goals were considered a good game.

The 26-0 "White Phantoms" "established Carolina as the team to beat," Shepard said. "It's been that way pretty consistently ever since."

Nobody's perfect; even the "White Phantoms" committed turnovers and missed shots. We all make mistakes every day. We botch our personal relationships; at work we seek competence, not perfection. To insist upon personal or professional perfection in our lives is to establish an impossibly high standard that eventually destroys us physically, emotionally, and mentally.

Yet that is exactly the standard God sets for us. Our love is to be perfect, never ceasing, never failing, never qualified – just the way God loves us. And Jesus didn't limit his command to only preachers and goody-two-shoes types. All of his disciples are to be perfect as they navigate their way through the world's ambiguous definition and understanding of love.

But that's impossible! Well, not necessarily if to love perfectly is to serve God wholeheartedly and to follow Jesus with single-minded devotion. Anyhow, in his perfect love for us, God makes allowance for our imperfect love and the consequences of it in the perfection of Jesus.

Practice does not make you perfect as nobody is perfect, but it does make you better.

--Soccer coach Adrian Parrish

**In his perfect love for us, God provides a way
for us to escape the consequences
of our imperfect love for him: Jesus.**

THE GOOD OLD DAYS

Read Psalm 102.

"My days vanish like smoke; . . . but you remain the same, and your years will never end" (vv. 3, 27).

Often we sigh and speak longingly of a return to the "good old days," but probably not when we're talking about college football.

Consider the day when players let their hair grow long for protection because they didn't wear helmets. The ball was shaped like a watermelon, too big to hold in your hand and pass. Games were called on account of darkness. A nose guard was about the only protection a player had. Maybe shoulder pads and hip pads, but only if he provided them himself.

Teams sometimes scrambled to find an opponent to play because no one scheduled any games. A slanted field rather than a level one. A player hid the ball under a jersey. No scoreboard. A player kicked a field goal by setting the ball on his helmet. The length of the halves was determined by agreement of the teams and usually depended upon the weather. Teammates dragged a tackled ball carrier forward. Linemen held hands and jumped to the right or to the left just before a play began.

This was the wild, wacky, and wooly game of college football in its early days, the 1890s and the turn of the century. UNC was part of those beginnings, fielding its first football team in 1888. Largely unregulated and unsophisticated with no forward pass, it was a game we would barely recognize today.

Thank goodness, we might well say. Given the symmetry, the excitement, the passion, and the sheer spectacle that surround today's college game, few, if any, Tar Heel fans would long for the days before Kenan Stadium when handles were sewn into the pants of ball carriers to make them easier to toss.

A longing for the "good old days" of your life springs from the brutal truth that time just never stands still. The current of your life sweeps you along until you realize one day you've lived long enough to have a past. Part of it you cling to fondly. The stunts you pulled with your high-school buddies. Your first apartment. That dance with your first love. That special vacation. Those "good old days."

You hold on relentlessly to the memory of those old, familiar ways because of the stability they provide in our uncertain world. They will always be there even as times change and you age.

Another constant exists in your life too. God has been a part of every event in your life that created a memory because he was there. He's always there with you; the question is whether you ignore him or make him a part of your day.

A "good old day" is any day shared with God.

Years ago, you used to get out and fight and run around and chase each other with a jackhammer and stuff like that. Those were the good old days.
                                    --Dale Earnhardt Jr. on NASCAR track etiquette

**Today is one of the "good old days"
if you share it with God.**

ANIMAL MAGNETISM

Read Psalm 139:1-18.

"For you created my inmost being; you knit me together in my mother's womb. I praise you because I am fearfully and wonderfully made" (vv. 13-14).

Strong, proud, and stubborn – those characteristics help to explain why the mascot of the North Carolina Tar Heels is a ram.

Actually a Horned Dorset Sheep, Rameses with his horns painted Carolina blue has been a part of the pageantry and color of North Carolina football since 1924 when cheerleader captain Vic Huggins came up with the idea of a ram for a mascot. According to Huggins, "In 1924 school spirit was at a peak. But something seemed to be missing. One day it hit me. Georgia had a bulldog for a mascot and (North Carolina) State a wolf. What Carolina needed was a symbol."

Huggins turned to UNC's recent football past for his inspiration. The star of the 9-1 1922 team had been a fullback named Jack Merritt, nicknamed "the battering ram" for the rugged way he pounded the line. Huggins took his idea to Charles T. Woollen, the athletic business manager. Woollen liked it and came up with $25 to purchase a ram for a mascot.

Huggins found what he wanted in Texas, and Rameses the First arrived in time for the VMI game of Nov. 8. The legendary events of the game ensured the ram would be UNC's permanent mascot. The teams slugged their way to a scoreless tie late in the fourth quarter when Carolina's Bunn Hackney was called on to try a field goal. Before he took the field, Hackney stopped and rubbed Rameses' head for good luck. His 30-yard kick was true, giving UNC the win.

More than eight decades later, the tradition continues with Rameses XVIII.

Impressive animals such as Rameses elicit our awe and our respect. Nothing enlivens a trip more than glimpsing turkeys, bears, or deer in the wild. Admit it: You go along with the kids' trip to the zoo because you think it's a cool place too. All that variety of life is mind-boggling. Who could conceive of a ram with its horns, a walrus, a moose, or a prairie dog? Who could possibly have that rich an imagination?

But the next time you're in a crowd, look around at the parade of faces. Who could come up with the idea for all those different people? For that matter, who could conceive of you? You are unique, a masterpiece who will never be duplicated.

The master creator, God Almighty, is behind it all. He thought of you and brought you into being. If you had a manufacturer's label, it might say, "Lovingly, fearfully, and wonderfully handmade in Heaven by #1 -- God."

His life has had an overt and lasting impact on the people whose lives he touched.
-- UNC AD Dick Baddour upon the 2007 death of Jason Ray, cheerleader who performed as the costumed Rameses

You may consider some painting or a magnificent animal a work of art, but the real masterpiece is you.

DAY 43

THOSE THINGS

Read Isaiah 55:6-13.

"For my thoughts are not your thoughts, neither are your ways my ways" (v. 8).

In the space of six seconds, he made two of the most important plays in Carolina basketball history. Then he fell victim to one of those things that happen in life and never played again.

When the Heels met Kansas and Wilt Chamberlain in the 1957 national championship game, junior Joe Quigg was the starting center and a solid pro prospect because he could score from outside. With ten points and nine rebounds, he was a key reason the underdog Tar Heels battled Kansas into triple overtime.

Then with six seconds left and Kansas leading 53-52, Quigg was fouled driving the lane. During a timeout, Quigg promised his teammates he would make both free throws. Coach Frank McGuire shared his confidence, instructing his players what they would do after – not if – Quigg made the shots.

He swished them both. But then the Heels blew the defense McGuire wanted, and the 6'7" Quigg found himself alone on the seven-foot Chamberlain. Sure enough, the pass came in, but Quigg leaped and deflected it to teammate Tommy Kearns. One of the most monumental games in collegiate basketball history was over, and Quigg had twice been the hero in the closing seconds.

Six months later, though, Quigg's basketball career effectively ended. In a Tar Heel practice before the season began, two teammates accidentally rolled on him from behind, breaking his right leg. "They kept me in a cast for six months," Quigg said. "That would never happen now, but that's the way it was treated back then. When the cast came off, my leg was all shriveled up. It couldn't bend."

Despite intense rehab, the leg never got better and Quigg never played again. It was just one of those things.

You've probably had a few of "those things" in your own life: bad breaks that occur without regard to justice, morality, or fair play. You wonder if everything in life is random with events determined by a chance roll of some cosmic dice. Is there really somebody scripting all this with logic and purpose?

Yes, there is; God is the author of everything.

We know how it all began; we even know how it all will end. It's in God's book. The part we play in God's kingdom, though, is in the middle, and that part is still being written. God is the author, and his ways are different from ours. After all he's God and we are not. That's why we don't know what's coming our way, and why "those things" catch us by surprise and dismay us when they do occur.

What God asks of us is that we trust him. He knows everything will be all right for those who follow Jesus.

Sometimes the calls go your way, and sometimes they don't.
-- Olympic gold medalist Dr. Dot Richardson

Life confounds us because, while we know the end and the beginning of God's great story, we are part of the middle, which God is still unfolding.

FACING THE MUSIC

Read Psalm 98.

"Sing to the Lord a new song, for he has done marvelous things" (v. 1).

If the Heels are playing, their loudest and most exuberant supporters will be a group that sits together and dresses alike: the UNC bands.

The original UNC band was formed in 1903 with its first public performance at a baseball game in 1904. About 275 students make up the marching band today; they also participate in the Basketball Bands and/or the Olympic Sport Pep Bands.

From the stands of Kenan Stadium, most of the band members who play the instruments are relatively anonymous, but for a time in the mid-1990s, one band member in particular stood out. He was a tuba player who was bald and wore half-glasses. A close examination also revealed he appeared more than slightly older than the other band members. He was: about 30 years older.

He was "Dr. Joe" Lowman, a UNC psychology professor who fulfilled a lifelong dream by marching in the band. "It was the only major regret of my life," he said. "That I didn't get to play in a big college marching band."

When Lowman turned 50 in the fall of 1994, his wife asked him what he wanted for his birthday. His answer was a complete surprise: a tuba. He had played in high school and had been good enough to win a replacement spot in the Charlotte symphony as a senior. His wife got used to "the low strains of the tuba wafting through the house" as he practiced. "At least," she said, "it's not drums, which he also plays."

His barber encouraged Lowman to chase his dream, and he asked UNC Bands Director Jim Hile if he could audition for a spot. He survived summer band camp with the rest of the kids (though he needed remedial walking lessons to improve his marching). In the fall of 1995 Dr. Joe Lowman was a full-fledged freshman band member, fulfilling a dream by making music.

Maybe you can't play a lick or carry a tune in the proverbial bucket. Or perhaps you do know your way around a guitar or a keyboard and can sing "Carolina on My Mind" on karaoke night without closing the joint down.

Unless you're a professional musician, however, how well you play or sing really doesn't matter. What counts is that you have music in your heart and sometimes you have to turn it loose.

Worshipping God has always included music in some form. That same boisterous and musical enthusiasm you exhibit when the Tar Heel Marching Band cranks up during a game should be a part of the joy you have in your personal worship of God.

When you consider that God loves you, he always will, and he has arranged through Jesus for you to spend eternity with him, how can that song God put in your heart not burst forth?

I never saw a college marching band without wishing that I had had the opportunity to play in one.

-- *Dr. Joe Lowman*

**You call it music; others may call it noise;
God calls it praise.**

DAY 45

GREAT EXPECTATIONS

Read John 1:43-51.

"'Nazareth! Can anything good come from there?'
Nathanael asked" (v. 46).

Pete Chilcutt was burdened with such low expectations when he arrived at Chapel Hill that Dean Smith asked him to take a redshirt.

Smith didn't often ask his players to take non-medical redshirts, but in Chilcutt's case he made an exception, so unimpressive was the skinny freshman. "For my first year or so at Carolina, my basketball future was going exactly nowhere," Chilcutt candidly admitted. "I had no idea what I was getting into," he said about playing basketball for Carolina. He quickly found out when he arrived in the fall of 1986, looked around, and saw "guys all over the place in my position." Before an exhibition game, Smith approached him and asked if he'd consider redshirting. "I agreed on the spot," Chilcutt said.

As it turned out, the rare move salvaged Chilcutt's rather unpromising career. While he at first tried to gain weight by eating every pizza he could find, he ultimately used the redshirt year to grow and to mature. From 1987-91, he played at 6'10" and 230 pounds. In 1991, with Chilcutt a senior captain along with Rick Fox and King Rice, the Heels advanced to the Final Four. He wound up scoring more than 1,100 points as a Tar Heel.

Chilcutt's first game may well have been his best. Against

top-ranked Syracuse in the season-opening Tip-off Classic, Chilcutt played most of the game because two players had been suspended. He scored 14 points, snared 13 rebounds, and hit a 10-footer as time expired to send the game into overtime. The Heels won 96-93.

This once-overmatched freshman about whom no one really had any expectations was taken in the first round of the NBA draft and had a nine-year career.

The blind date your friend promised would look like Brad Pitt or Jennifer Aniston but resembled a Munster. Your vacation that went downhill after the lost luggage. Often your expectations are raised only to be dashed. Sometimes it's best not to get your hopes up; then at least you have the possibility of being surprised.

Worst of all, perhaps, is when you realize that you are the one not meeting others' expectations. The fact is, though, that you aren't here to live up to what others think of you. Jesus didn't; in part, that's why they killed him. But he did meet God's expectations for his life, which was all that really mattered.

Because God's kingdom is so great, God does have great expectations for any who would enter, and you should not take them lightly. What the world expects from you is of no importance; what God expects from you is paramount.

Other people may not have had high expectations for me, but I had high expectations for myself.
-- Gymnast Shannon Miller

**You have little if anything to gain from meeting
the world's expectations of you; you have all
of eternity to gain from meeting God's.**

DAY 46

STRANGE BUT TRUE

Read 1 Corinthians 1:18-31.

"The message of the cross is foolishness to those who are perishing, but to us who are being saved it is the power of God" (v. 18).

Perhaps the strangest football game in UNC history was the 1949 contest against Duke: It ended twice.

The game was strange even before it began when the Tar Heel buses got tied up in traffic and the players arrived only minutes before the scheduled 2 p.m. kickoff. Duke scored on the first play from scrimmage, but Ed Bilpuch and All-American Ken Powell blocked the extra point attempt.

Limping on an ankle injury suffered in the first quarter, Charlie Justice threw two touchdown passes to All-American end Art Weiner and caught a TD pass from Billy Hayes to give UNC a 21-6 lead in the third quarter.

Duke rallied, though, pulling to within one point with 2:55 left and then moving to the Carolina 20 with only a few seconds left. That's when everything really got strange.

The Blue Devils threw an incomplete pass, and as Weiner explained it, "As soon as the ball hit the ground, the clock was supposed to stop. But some official inadvertently let the clock go on and then signaled the end of the game." Thousands of jubilant Carolina fans and disappointed Duke fans poured onto the field, and some of the players headed to the dressing rooms.

But Duke coaches argued with the referee that the clock should have stopped, giving the Blue Devils time for one more play. They won their point. "It took police and grounds keepers and a frenzied appeal from the public address system about five minutes to clear the field," said one paper.

The second ending didn't change anything. Weiner blocked a Duke field goal attempt to preserve the strange but true 21-20 Carolina win.

Life is just strange, isn't it? How else to explain the college bowl situation, Dr. Phil, tattoos, curling, tofu, and teenagers? Isn't it strange that today we have more ways to stay in touch with each other yet are losing the intimacy of personal contact?

And how strange is it that God let himself be killed by being nailed to a couple of pieces of wood? Think about that: the creator and ruler of the entire universe suffering the indignity and the torture that he did. And he did it quite willingly; this was God, after all. It's not like he wasn't capable of changing the course of events -- but he didn't. Isn't that strange?

But there's more that's downright bewildering. The cross, a symbol of disgrace, defeat, and death, ultimately became a worldwide symbol of hope, victory, and life. That's really strange. So is the fact that love drove God to that cross. It's strange – but it's true.

It was a real strange thing. . . . Nobody laid a hand on me.
  -- Art Weiner on his field-goal block that ended the '49 Duke game

It's strange but true: God allowed himself to be killed on a cross because of his great love for you.

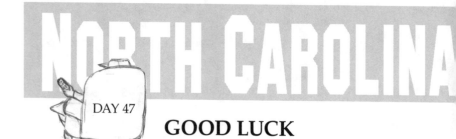
DAY 47

GOOD LUCK

Read 1 Samuel 28:3-20.

"Saul then said to his attendants, 'Find me a woman who is a medium, so I may go and inquire of her'" (v. 7).

From wolfing down Paydays to spitting in the river, Tar Heel assistant coach Roy Williams went above and beyond his usual coaching duties to help the 1982 team win the national title.

According to senior point guard Jimmy Black, Williams was one of the most superstitious members of the team. Williams coached the JV team and often didn't have enough time between the JV game and the varsity game to grab himself something to eat. An usher helped him out after a couple of the JV games early in the championship season by giving Williams a candy bar to tide him over. The Heels won both games.

On Jan. 21, 1982, though, the candy man wasn't at the game, and Williams didn't get his candy bar. Wake Forest upset UNC 55-48. That clinched it for Williams; before every game from then on, he had to have a candy bar even if it meant scrambling to a concession stand. Otherwise, the Heels were doomed. His favorites were Payday, Zero, and Fifth Avenue.

Candy wasn't Williams' only superstition in New Orleans, site of the Final Four. He heard that it was good luck to spit in the Mississippi River. "I'm a jogger and I wanted some exercise, so the morning of the Houston game (the semifinals), I went jogging and spat in the river," Williams said. Doing all he could to help the cause, when he returned to the hotel lobby, Williams told everyone he met -- including sophomore forward Matt Doherty's family – about his addition to the river's water level. "Well, I've done my part," Williams declared.

By the time of the championship game, Williams had a whole bunch of folks – including the entire Doherty family – loading up and spitting into the river.

Black cats are right pretty. A medium is a steak. A key chain with a rabbit's foot wasn't too lucky for the rabbit. And what in the world is a blarney stone? About as superstitious as you get is to say "God bless you" when somebody sneezes.

You look indulgently upon good-luck charms, tarot cards, astrology, palm readers, and the like; they're really just amusing and harmless. So what's the problem? Nothing as long as you conduct yourself with the belief that superstitious objects and rituals – from broken mirrors to your daily horoscope –can't bring about good or bad luck. You aren't willing to let such notions and nonsense rule your life.

The danger of superstition lies in its ability to lure you into trusting it, thus allowing it some degree of influence over your life. In that case, it subverts God's rightful place.

Whether or not it's superstition, something does rule your life. It should be God – and God alone.

I don't believe in a jinx or a hex. Winning depends on how well you block and tackle.

-- *Shug Jordan*

Superstitions may not rule your life, but something does; it should be God and God alone.

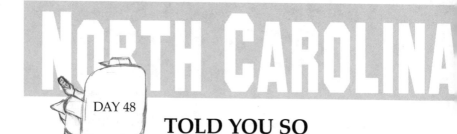
DAY 48

TOLD YOU SO

Read Matthew 24:15-31.

"See, I have told you ahead of time" (v. 25).

On the night of April 5, 1993, Donald Williams could well have said, "I told you so."

That was the night Williams led the Tar Heels to a 77-71 win over Michigan and the national championship.

His friends had meant well when they told Williams he wasn't good enough to play at North Carolina, that he would only sit on the bench, and that he should go to N.C. State instead.

Williams' freshman season of 1991-92 made those naysayers look right. This highly recruited, high-scoring, high school All-America whom one writer called the best 3-point shooting freshman in the country sat on the bench just like those folks had said he would. He played behind Derrick Phelps and averaged only 2.2 points per game.

That nondescript season lowered expectations for Williams' sophomore season. The 14-page UNC media guide's preview of the 1992-93 team mentioned him only once, and even that was less than promising: "(Henrik) Rodl, (Scott) Cherry and Williams will all get long looks at" the shooting guard position vacated by the departure of Hubert Davis.

But Williams listened to those who encouraged him rather than those who clucked "I told you so." By midseason, he was the starting shooting guard. He averaged 14.3 points per game, behind only Eric Montross and George Lynch.

He saved his best for the Final Four, setting three shooting records including most 3-pointers made (10). He led the team with 25 points in the semifinal win over Kansas and then duplicated the feat in the finals.

He was the Final Four MVP, a message sent forth loud and clear: "I told you so."

Don't you just hate it in when somebody says, "I told you so"? That means the other person was right and you were wrong; that other person has spoken the truth. You could have listened to that know-it-all in the first place, but then you would have lost the chance yourself to crow, "I told you so."

In our pluralistic age and society, many view truth as relative, meaning absolute truth does not exist. All belief systems have equal value and merit. But this is a ghastly, dangerous fallacy because it ignores the truth that God proclaimed in the presence and words of Jesus.

In speaking the truth, Jesus told everybody exactly what he was going to do: come back and take his faithful with him. Those who don't listen or who don't believe will be left behind with those four awful words, "I told you so," ringing in their ears and wringing their souls.

There's nothing in this world more instinctively abhorrent to me than finding myself in agreement with my fellow humans.
-- Lou Holtz

Jesus matter-of-factly told us what he has planned:
He will return to gather all the faithful to himself.

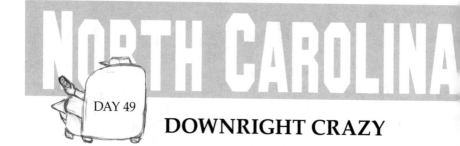
DAY 49

DOWNRIGHT CRAZY

Read Luke 13:31-35.

"Some Pharisees came to Jesus and said to him, 'Leave this place and go somewhere else. Herod wants to kill you.' He replied, 'Go tell that fox . . . I must keep going today and tomorrow and the next day'" (vv. 31-33).

Any rational, knowledgeable student of collegiate soccer would say the very idea is crazy, that it could never happen. But it did. UNC's Yael Averbuch scored a goal four seconds into a match.

Averbuch completed her UNC career in 2008 as a three-time All-America and the national player of the year as a sophomore in 2006. She was the ACC Women's Soccer Scholar Athlete of the Year in 2008 and set an NCAA record by starting 105 straight matches at UNC.

On Sept. 3, 2006, against Yale, midfielder Averbuch delivered a 55-yard bomb that sailed past the startled Yalie goalkeeper four seconds into the match, the fastest goal in NCAA history and one of those records not likely ever to be broken.

It's so crazy it had to be an accident, but it wasn't really. Averbuch said she could boom a ball 70 yards with her right foot and 60 with her left. Her power resulted from hours of practice. As a young player, she visited a nearby schoolyard and spent hours kicking a ball against a wall, alternating her feet. So the distance of the kick and the power with which it was made weren't flukes.

Neither was the fact that she attempted the kick at all. In

pregame talks, the Heels discussed the possibility of taking a shot if the Yale goalkeeper wandered a bit. At the opening whistle, Averbuch took a look, and sure enough the keeper was off her line. "I thought, 'What the hey?'" Averbuch said, and so she let fly. "Obviously I didn't expect to score a goal on it," Averbuch said, but the goalkeeper couldn't get back in time to reach the kick.

Four seconds and a "golly-gee-wow" clip that ESPN ran repeatedly. Just downright crazy.

What some see as ridiculous or crazy often is shrewd instead. Like Yael Averbuch's kick, which wasn't really happenstance at all. Or like the time you went into business for yourself or when you decided to go back to school. Maybe it was when you fixed up that old house. Or when you bought that new company's stock.

You know a good thing when you see it but are also shrewd enough to spot something that's downright crazy. Jesus was that way too. He knew that entering Jerusalem was in complete defiance of all apparent reason and logic since a whole bunch of folks who wanted to kill him were waiting for him there.

Nevertheless, he went because he also knew that when the great drama had played out he would defeat not only his personal enemies but the most fearsome enemy of all: death itself.

It was, after all, a shrewd move that provided the way to your salvation.

Football is easy if you're crazy.

-- Bo Jackson

It's so good it sounds crazy -- but it's not: through faith in Jesus, you can have eternal life with God.

THE BIG TIME

Read Matthew 2:19-23.

"He went and lived in a town called Nazareth" (v. 23).

Once upon a time, not many folks paid attention to Tar Heel basketball or even cared too much about it.

In 1952, football was king on the Chapel Hill campus. Basketball in the state "was a cult sport." Oh, UNC had had its moments: the national title in 1924 awarded retroactively and a 1946 appearance in the NCAA title game. By 1952, though, North Carolina State under Everett Case ruled the state in basketball and routinely buried the Heels. The reason was simple: NC State "took the sport of basketball more seriously than many of their competitors," including UNC. When UNC's head basketball coach Tom Scott resigned in 1952, barely anyone noticed.

Then in August 1952, UNC made its first stride toward a permanent place in the big time by hiring Frank McGuire. That eventually led to the historic night of Dec. 14, 1955, more than a year removed from the national championship of 1957, when the University of North Carolina officially kicked down the door to big-time basketball.

Heading into the 1955-56 season, McGuire had managed to make Carolina respectable, but that was about all with records of 17-10, 11-10, and 10-11. Still, the Heels were ranked 16th when they hosted 5th-ranked Alabama in a game that created so much buzz even the *New York Times* sent a reporter. The storyline was that the game would let UNC see how far it had to go to move into the big time. The answer was resoundingly clear: The Heels had arrived.

They smashed Alabama 99-77. The rather prescient *Times* reporter wrote, "Mark down North Carolina as next year's NCAA champions." Big-time basketball was here to stay in Chapel Hill.

The move to the big time is one we often desire to make in our own lives. Bumps in the road, one stoplight communities, and towns with only a service station, a church, and a voting place litter the American countryside. Maybe you were born in one of them and grew up in a virtually unknown village in a backwater county. Perhaps you started out on a stage far removed from the bright lights of Broadway, the glitz of Hollywood, or the halls of power in Washington, D.C.

Those original circumstances don't have to define or limit you, though, for life is much more than geography. It is about character and walking with God whether you're in the countryside or the city.

Jesus knew the truth of that. After all, he grew up in a small town in an inconsequential region of an insignificant country ruled by foreign invaders.

Where you are doesn't matter. What you are does.

I live so far out in the country that I have to walk toward town to go hunting.
-- Former major leaguer Rocky Bridges

**Where you live may largely be the culmination
of a series of circumstances;
what you are is a choice you make.**

DAY 51

PRESSURE COOKER

Read 1 Kings 18:16-40.

"Answer me, O Lord, answer me, so these people will know that you, O Lord, are God" (v. 37).

No athlete in Carolina history ever faced more pressure than [Charlie] Scott when he enrolled here."

By any standard, Scott's time at UNC from 1967-70 was a rousing success. After a season on the freshman team, Scott played in the shadow of Larry Miller as a sophomore before exploding onto the national consciousness his junior season. He averaged 22 points a game as a junior and 27 as a senior, leading the Heels both seasons to ACC titles and Final Four berths.

A two-time All-America and three-time All-ACC selection, Scott finished his career as the second leading scorer in Carolina history, only 38 points behind Lennie Rosenbluth. Dean Smith said of Scott his senior season, he was "the best all-around player in the country."

Playing at UNC comes with its own very special brand of pressure, so what made Scott's time in the limelight so different?

He was the first African-American scholarship athlete to play at Chapel Hill, so he carried on his back more than the expectations that came with being highly recruited. From Harlem, Scott decided to make the radical move of playing college basketball in the South because of the enthusiasm for the sport he saw there. When he visited Chapel Hill, he took a walk through town without the coaches. "Everybody was nice to him," Smith recalled. "He said he felt like he belonged."

Life as a pioneer wasn't easy, though. Scott was the target of open bitterness and hatred on the road. He received "ugly racial threats" in the mail. "The fact that he was black and was the first of his race here certainly put him on the spot," said Jack Williams, former UNC sports information director.

As Charlie Scott did at UNC and as Elijah did so long ago, you live every day with pressure. You lay it on the line with everybody watching. Your family, coworkers, or employees – they depend on you. You know the pressure of a deadline, of a job evaluation, of taking the risk of asking someone to go out with you, of driving in rush-hour traffic.

Help in dealing with daily pressure is readily available, and the only price you pay for it is your willingness to believe. God will give you the grace to persevere if you ask prayerfully.

And while you may need some convincing, the pressures of daily living are really small potatoes because they all will pass. The real pressure comes in deciding where you will spend eternity because that decision is forever. You can handle that pressure easily enough by deciding for Jesus. Eternity is then taken care of; the pressure's off – forever.

It was pretty bad. If our fans acted that way toward a visiting player, I would be ashamed of it.
-- Charlie Scott on his harassment during road games

The greatest pressure you face in life
concerns where you will spend eternity,
which can be dealt with by deciding for Jesus.

DAY 52

THE SIMPLE LIFE

Read 1 John 1:5-10.

"If we confess our sins, he is faithful and just and will forgive us our sins and purify us from all unrighteousness" (v. 9).

Trailing 15-10, the Heels were 61 yards away from the Duke goal line with only 1:42 left. Coach Dick Crum had a simple formula to ensure a win: Give the ball to Famous Amos.

The ACC Rookie of the Year in 1977, Amos Lawrence had four straight seasons in which he rushed for more than 1,000 yards. His 4,391 yards rushing is still the Carolina record as is his 25 games of at least 100 yards rushing. In 1977 and 1980, Lawrence was first-team All-ACC; two publications named him All-America in 1980.

On Nov. 25, 1978, Duke came to Kenan Stadium for the season finale of Crum's first year and seemed to have the game under control with a 15-3 lead late in the fourth quarter. With three minutes left, though, the Heels scored and the defense forced a punt. To win, however, UNC would have to navigate 61 yards with no timeouts. Crum turned to Lawrence three times during the drive when a big play was needed.

On third and twelve from the Carolina 37, quarterback Matt Kupec surprised Duke by handing off to Lawrence, who broke two tackles on his way to an 18-yard gain and a first down. Then on fourth and one at the Duke 36, Crum called a draw, and

TAR HEELS

Lawrence rambled for 19 yards as the clock ticked to under 30 seconds. Only 18 seconds remained when UNC faced third down at the Duke 12. Kupec again gave the ball to Lawrence in what would be the game's last play unless he scored. Lawrence hit one defender, eluded another, and danced into the end zone.

Dick Crum's simple formula yielded a 16-15 UNC win.

Perhaps the simple life in America was doomed by the arrival of the programmable VCR. Since then, we've been on an inevitably downward spiral into ever more complicated lives. Even windshield wipers have multiple settings now, and it takes a graduate degree to figure out clothes dryers.

But we might do well in our own lives to mimic the simple approach Dick Crum employed to beat Duke. That is, we should approach our lives with the keen awareness that success requires simplicity, a sticking to the basics: Revere God, love our families, honor our country, do our best.

Theologians may make what God did in Jesus complicated and bewildering, but God kept it simple for us: believe, trust, and obey. Believe in Jesus as the Son of God, trust that through him God makes possible our deliverance from our sins into Heaven, and obey God in the way he wants us to live. It's simple, but it's the true winning formula, the way to win for all eternity.

I think God made it simple. Just accept Him and believe.
-- Bobby Bowden

Life continues to get ever more complicated,
but God made it simple for us
when he showed up as Jesus.

DAY 53

TEACHER'S PET

Read John 3:1-16.

"[Nicodemus] came to Jesus at night and said, 'Rabbi, we know you are a teacher who has come from God'" (v. 2).

When Mike Fox was hired in 1998 to take the UNC baseball program to new levels, one of the first persons to welcome him home was one of his former teachers. Guy named Dean Smith.

Fox was a three-time baseball letterman in the mid-70s, hitting .277 as a senior second baseman. Before that, though, Fox pursued his first love as a walk-on point guard on the Heels' JV basketball squad. Without intentionally doing so, he became the JV team's coach on the floor. He studied the varsity's practices under Smith, "noting precise workout schedules, remembering 'thoughts of the day,' respecting discipline." "I can remember my first couple times [at varsity practice]," Fox recalled, "and I was just like, 'This might be the greatest thing, ever.' . . . That's most definitely when the coaching bug hit me."

Fortunately for the future of the UNC baseball program, Phil Ford stood between Fox and the varsity. Wisely, Fox decided to concentrate on baseball, which he coached after graduation with "the lessons he had learned on the Carmichael Court . . . super-glued to his brain." "[For] kids that are exposed to North Carolina basketball," explained former Smith assistant Eddie Fogler, "it's like an academic course. . . . It doesn't surprise me that he's become such a good coach."

TAR HEELS

Shortly after he returned to Chapel Hill, Fox and his son ran into Smith and his grandchildren outside the Smith Center. They shot some hoops for a while, a time Fox said "might have been the coolest 2½ hours I've ever spent." Time spent with his basketball teacher, from whom he learned the lessons he now teaches so well to his baseball players.

You can read this book, break 90 on the golf course, and be successful at your job because somebody taught you. And as you learn, you become the teacher yourself. You teach your children how to play Monopoly and how to drive a car. You show rookies the ropes at the office and teach baseball's basics to a Little League team.

This pattern of learning and then teaching includes your spiritual life also. Somebody taught you about Jesus, and this, too, you must pass on. Jesus came to teach a truth the religious teachers and the powerful of his day did not want to hear. Little has changed in that regard, as the world today often reacts with scorn and disdain to Jesus' message.

Nothing, not even death itself, could stop Jesus from teaching his lesson of life and salvation. So should nothing stop you from teaching life's most important lesson: Jesus saves.

The only reason we make good role models is because you guys look up to athletes. . . . The real role models should be your parents and teachers!
-- NFL player Dante Hall

In life, you lean and then you teach,
which includes learning and teaching about Jesus,
the most important lesson of all.

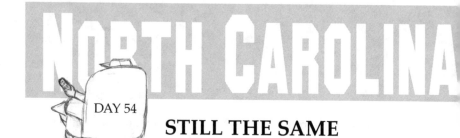

DAY 54

STILL THE SAME

Read Hebrews 13:5-16.

"Jesus Christ is the same yesterday and today and forever" (v. 8).

College basketball at Chapel Hill isn't what it used to be.

In the early part of the twentieth century, for instance, scheduling of games was haphazard. One of those pioneering Tar Heel players, Roy McKnight, remembered that "we just picked up games as we could." As a result, North Carolina played some of the usual suspects such as Wake Forest and Virginia, but also regularly played a team from the Durham YMCA.

The early coaches knew so little about basketball that the players virtually coached themselves. The first coach, Nat Cartmell, was a track man; his successor, Charles Doak, was a baseball coach.

The squad was filled through open tryouts. In 1917, for example, a sign appeared on campus calling all men wishing to try out to report to Bynum gym. The sign enticed students with the promises they could "learn to pass, dribble and shoot the goal [and] earn a place on the squad and the training table."

The game was much rougher back then. "Today's players would be lucky to last 10 minutes in the tempo and temperament of our times," declared Raby Tennent, who played from 1913-17, the last year as the team captain. "It was truly the survival of the fittest. Broken noses, flips, knockdowns, and people carried out on stretchers" all characterized the game, according to Tennent.

The scores were much lower in those early days than they are today. Tennent was widely recognized as a "defensive genius," allowing only eighteen goals the entire season of 1916-17. The ball contributed to the low scores; it was so heavy the players had to use two hands to shoot and couldn't dribble much.

Like everything else in your life, basketball at UNC and the game itself have changed with the years. Computers and CDs, cell phones and George Foreman grills, Mexican restaurants and IMAX theaters – they and much that is in your life now may not have even been around when you were 16. Think about how style, cars, communications, and tax laws constantly change.

Don't be too harsh on the world, though, because you've changed also. You've aged, gained or lost weight, gotten married, changed jobs, or relocated.

Have you ever found yourself bewildered by the rapid pace of change, casting about for something to hold on to that will always be the same, that you can use as an anchor for your life? Is there anything like that?

Sadly, the answer's no. All the things of this world change.

On the other hand, there's Jesus, who is the same today, the same forever, always dependable, always loving you. No matter what happens in your life, Jesus is still the same.

We played an aggressive, fast, rough-and-tumble game. Scores were in the 30s and 40s.

-- Raby Tennent on early UNC basketball

In our ever-changing and bewildering world,
Jesus is the same forever;
his love for you will never change.

DAY 55

JUMPING FOR JOY

Read Luke 6:20-26.

"Rejoice in that day and leap for joy, because great is your reward in heaven" (v. 23).

Billy Cunningham wasn't nicknamed the Kangaroo Kid for nothing; he could flat jump.

The two-time All-America arrived in Chapel Hill from Brooklyn in 1962, Dean Smith's first season as head coach. He was a prolific scorer, leading the ACC in scoring in 1964 and '65 and averaging 24.8 points per game as a Tar Heel. Against Tulane in 1964, he set a Carolina record with 48 points.

Cunningham's collegiate career was defined, however, by "his uncanny leaping ability." He led the ACC in rebounds all three years he played varsity ball. His 1,062 career rebounds, 379 rebounds in 1964, and rebound average of 16.1 per game in 1963 were all school records at the time.

Standing 6'6", Cunningham earned his colorful moniker as the Kangaroo Kid after he outjumped a 7-foot Duke player his freshman season. His sophomore season Cunningham stunned Notre Dame with a shot from midcourt that tied the game at the buzzer; he led all scorers with 26 points as UNC won in overtime. All of which led the Notre Dame coach to declare Cunningham to be "the best rebounder I've seen in a long time."

Ken Rappaport said Cunningham "stood on pencil-thin legs wrapped in baggy socks . . . and when he went up for a rebound, the socks went down and the jersey flopped out. He was anything but poetry." But sportswriter Bob Quincy noted that Cunningham consistently outjumped players six inches taller.

He was so good that Smith was forced to play him out of position, at center, which fitted neither Cunningham's size nor his temperament. As a result, Smith said, Cunningham "never really got his full opportunity in college." But the Kangaroo Kid never complained. He just kept jumping.

You're probably a pretty good jumper yourself when UNC hits a basket in the last seconds against Duke. You just can't help it. It's like your feet and your seat have suddenly become magnets that repel each other. The sad part is that you always come back down to earth; the moment of exultation passes.

But what if you could jump for joy all the time? Not literally, of course; you'd pass out from exhaustion. But figuratively, with your heart aglow and joyous even when life is its most difficult.

Joy is an absolutely essential component of the Christian life. Not only do we experience joy in our public praise and worship – which is temporary – but we live daily in the joy that comes from the presence of God in our lives and the surety of his saving power extended to us through Jesus Christ.

It's not happiness, which derives from external factors; it's joy, which comes from inside.

I could always jump.

-- Billy Cunningham

**Unbridled joy can send you jumping all
over the place; life in Jesus means such exultation
is not rare but rather is a way of life.**

DAY 56

BLIND JUSTICE

Read Micah 6:6-8.

"He has showed you, O man, what is good. And what does the Lord require of you? To act justly and to love mercy and to walk humbly with your God" (v. 8).

Two wrongs don't make a right -- except for the night of Oct. 11, 2008 – when justice was ultimately served and the Heels took a heartpounding and somewhat bizarre win over Notre Dame.

Before the third-largest crowd in Kenan Stadium history, the Irish led 24-22 until quarterback Cam Sexton hurdled into the end zone on the first play of the fourth quarter to give the Heels their first lead of the night. Lineman Aleric Mullins had set up the score by causing and recovering a fumble on a quarterback sack.

When the clock rolled under two minutes, the "wrongs" showed up.

First wrong: With 1:57 left, Brooks Foster hauled in a pass at the Notre Dame 23 that gave UNC a first down and a chance to run out the clock. Though the replay clearly showed Foster had the ball, the replay official overturned the ruling on the field. UNC had to punt, giving Notre Dame a chance to pull it out.

Which it looked as though the Irish would do until:

Second wrong. With less than ten seconds left, officials made what seemed to be the correct call when they ruled a ND pass to the Carolina seven complete with the receiver down by contact before Jordan Hemby stripped the ball and Trimane Goddard recovered for the Heels. Again, though, the replay folks struck, ruling the play was a completed pass and a fumble. Instead of Notre Dame, UNC got the last play. Sexton took a knee.

"It's a bitter ending," Notre Dame's Charlie Weis said. UNC Coach Butch Davis said he couldn't recall a more bizarre game.

Justice won out, though, as two wrongs made a right and the Heels had a big 29-24 win.

Where's the justice when cars fly past you as a state trooper pulls you over? When the refs blow a call? When a con man swindles an elderly neighbor? When crooked politicians treat your tax dollars as a personal slush fund? When children starve?

Injustice enrages us, but anger by itself is not enough. The establishment of justice in this world has to start with each one of us. The Lord requires it of us. For most of us, a just world is one in which everybody gets what he or she deserves.

But that is not God's way. God expects us to be just and merciful in all our dealings without consideration as to whether the other person "deserves" it. The justice we dispense should truly be blind.

If that doesn't sound "fair," then pause and consider that when we stand before God, the last thing we want is what we deserve. We want mercy, not justice.

None of us wants justice from God. What we want is mercy because if we got justice, we'd all go to hell.
-- Bobby Bowden

God requires that we dispense justice and mercy without regards to deserts, exactly what we pray we will in turn receive from God.

DAY 57

THE SUB

Read Galatians 3:10-14.

*"Christ redeemed us from the curse of the law by
becoming a curse for us" (v. 13).*

One of the greatest coaches in college basketball history was
not one of the game's greatest players. In fact, Dean Smith's lot at
the University of Kansas was as a sub.

Smith spent two seasons (1951-53) on the KU varsity with most
of the time spent on the bench. The 1951-52 team won the NCAA
championship, and the 1952-53 squad lost in the finals. In the
80-63 championship win over St. John's, Smith played for thirty
seconds and wasn't even included in the box score. In the 69-68
loss to Indiana in 1953, he hit one free throw and committed one
foul.

Smith averaged fewer than two points a game for his KU career,
but he took advantage of the pine time as his teammates and he
would talk strategy while the game was in progress. Former
Smith teammate B.H. Born said he and the legend-in-the-making
would discuss what could be changed to make the team better."
They had a lot of time to do it as in 1951-52 "neither of us played
much until the game was decided."

Why didn't Smith see more playing time? As he was more
than once described at subsequent team reunions, Smith was the
prototypical coach: too small and too slow. Smith himself confessed that he was no leaper either. Born said his teammate was

"a good ballhandler who played fierce defense." He didn't shoot much, scoring 25 field goals in his two seasons on the varsity.

Smith compensated for his athletic shortcomings by developing an affinity for "the cerebral side of the game." As history went on to reveal, the KU sub managed that part of the game very, very well.

Wouldn't it be cool if you had a substitute for all of life's hard stuff? Telling of a death in the family? Call in your sub. Breaking up with your boyfriend? Job interview? Chemistry test? Crucial presentation at work? Let the sub handle it.

We do have such a substitute, but not for the matters of life. Instead, Jesus is our substitute for the much more important matters of life and death. Since Jesus has already made it, we don't have to make the sacrifice God demands for forgiveness and salvation.

One of the ironies of our age is that many people desperately grope for a substitute for Jesus. Mysticism, human philosophies such as Scientology, false religions such as Hinduism and Islam, cults, New Age approaches that preach self-fulfillment without responsibility or accountability – they and others like them are all pitiful, inadequate substitutes for Jesus.

Accept no substitutes. It's Jesus or nothing.

I never substitute just to substitute. The only way a guy gets off the floor is if he dies.

– Former basketball coach Abe Lemons

**There is no substitute for Jesus,
the consummate substitute.**

DAY 58

DRY RUN

Read John 4:1-14.

"Everyone who drinks this water will be thirsty again,
but whoever drinks the water I give him will never thirst.
Indeed, the water I give him will become in him a spring
of water welling up to eternal life" (vv. 13-14).

The drought was of biblical proportions; it lasted almost ten years.

On Oct. 18, 1992, the Tar Heels of Coach Mack Brown upset 17th-ranked Virginia 27-7, marking the first defeat of a ranked team since the 26-10 win over Texas in the 1982 Sun Bowl.

The defense led the way holding the nation's pass-efficiency leader to only 11 for 25 for a pitiful 102 yards with two interceptions. The offense didn't exactly sit around and watch. Junior Natrone Means -- a two-time All-ACC tailback who would turn pro after the season and whose career rushing total of 3,074 yards remains the sixth best in Carolina history -- ran for 216 yards. When sophomore quarterback Jason Stanicek went down with a knee injury, freshman Mike Thomas kept the offense moving.

Virginia went 75 yards on its first possession to lead 7-0, but the game belonged to the Heels after that. A Tripp Pignetti field goal, a 37-yard TD pass from Stanicek to split end Corey Holliday, and a 17-yard run from Randy Jordan made it 17-7 at halftime. From then on, the defense made sure the drought would be broken.

Just for good measure, the Heels repeated the feat the following week when they defeated 19th-ranked Georgia Tech 26-14, a win that inspired the crowd to tear down the goal posts. The double dip marked the first time in UNC football history the Heels had beaten ranked opponents on successive weekends.

"I was just running around crazy," said senior fullback Mike Faulkerson about the post-game celebration. "I looked up and saw the fans tearing down the goalposts, and I just said, 'Wow!'"

That pretty much said it all about the ending of the drought.

You can walk across that river you boated on in the spring. The city's put all neighborhoods on water restriction, and that beautiful lawn you fertilized and seeded will turn a sickly, pale green and may lapse all the way to brown. Somebody wrote "Wash Me" on the rear window of your truck.

The sun bakes everything, including the concrete. The earth itself seems exhausted, just barely hanging on. It's a drought.

It's the way a soul looks that shuts God out.

God instilled thirst in us to warn us of our body's need for physical water. He also gave us a spiritual thirst that can be quenched only by his presence in our lives. Without God, we are like tumbleweeds, dried out and windblown, offering the illusion of life where there is only death.

Living water – water of life – is readily available in Jesus. We may drink our fill, and thus we slake our thirst and end our soul's drought – forever.

Drink before you are thirsty. Rest before you are tired.
-- Paul de Vivie, father of French cycle touring

Our soul thirsts for God's refreshing presence.

DAY 59

DO WHAT YOU HAVE TO

Read 2 Samuel 12:1-15a.

"The Lord sent Nathan to David" (v. 1).

Dean Smith did what he had to, not what he wanted to. The result was a player who led Carolina to a sensational season and went on to have one of pro basketball's great careers.

Among Smith's basic tenets was that he didn't recruit junior college players. It had to do with the way he built his program. "It's a seniority thing," explained a person close to UNC. "You work your way up. He doesn't think it's fair to bring someone in and put him ahead of a guy who played here as a freshman."

Smith found himself shorthanded, though, after a recruiting war for Tom McMillen in 1970. The 6'11"-McMillen publicly announced he was going to Carolina. "He was going to be [Smith's] big man. He had counted on a big man," said an observer. The week before school started in September, though, Smith received a telegram that said simply, "Going to Maryland for reasons you know. Tom McMillen."

Smith unexpectedly was left without his big man and without time to develop one, so he went the junior college route and found Bob McAdoo, a 6'9" "slender, soft-spoken giant" from Greensboro who had led Vincennes (Indiana) Junior College to the national championship. McAdoo helped the Heels to a 26-5 season in 1971-72 that included the ACC championship and a berth in the NCAA semifinals. He led the team in scoring (19.5) and rebounding (10.1) and was first-team All-America, All-ACC, and the ACC Tournament MVP. He was also an all-tournament selection for the East Regional and the Final Four.

McAdoo turned pro after his one season at Chapel Hill and went on to a career that eventually landed him in the Naismith Basketball Hall of Fame, one of eight Tar Heels to be so honored.

Like Dean Smith and his junior college player, you've had to do some things in your life that you really didn't want to do. Maybe when you put your daughter on severe restriction, broke the news of a death in the family, fired a friend, or underwent surgery. You plowed ahead because you knew it was for the best or you had no choice.

Nathan surely didn't want to confront King David and tell him what a miserable reprobate he'd been, but the prophet had no choice: Obedience to God overrode all other factors. Of all that God asks of us in the living of a godly life, obedience is perhaps the most difficult. After all, our history of disobedience stretches all the way back to the Garden of Eden.

The problem is that God expects obedience not only when his wishes match our own but also when they don't. Obedience to God is a way of life, not a matter of convenience.

Coaching is making men do what they don't want, so they can become what they want to be.
-- Legendary NFL Coach Tom Landry

You can never foresee what God will demand of you, but obedience requires being ready to do whatever God asks.

DAY 60

SHAPE UP

Read Luke 12:35-40.

"You also must be ready, because the Son of Man will come at an hour when you do not expect him" (v. 40).

One thing you can say about the UNC football team of 1895: They were in shape.

The squad's 7-1-1 record was the best to date. The lone loss was 6-0 to Virginia at Richmond, but the home crowd was really the deciding factor, twice running onto the field and blocking Carolina runners on their way to touchdowns.

The season was unusual for other reasons too. Lore has it that on Saturday, Oct. 27, 1895, in the game against Georgia, the Tar Heels threw the first forward pass in college football history. The legendary John Heisman himself declared this to be so. According to Heisman, a UNC punt was about to be blocked when the desperate punter dashed to his right and tossed the ball to George Stephens, who ran 70 yards for the game's only touchdown. The pass was illegal, but it stood despite the protestations of the Georgia coach, Pop Warner.

Then there was the matter of the team being in shape. It had to be because the Heels of '95 endured the most grueling road trip in Carolina football history. A squad of only fifteen players left Chapel Hill the afternoon of Friday, Oct. 26, arrived in Atlanta the next morning, and whipped Georgia that afternoon with that famous forward pass. The team hit the rails again and beat Vanderbilt

12-0 in Nashville on Monday, tied Sewanee 0-0 at Sewanee on Tuesday, and then returned to Atlanta to beat Georgia again 10-6 on Wednesday. Coach T.C. Trenchard "doubled as a trainer on the train ride back to Chapel Hill, unceasingly massaging his players with liniment and hot water."

Said one observer, "This was the tiredest group of football players in the United States." To endure such a grueling regimen and still win, Trenchard's men had to be in great shape.

Like a long football season with its share of road trips, life is an endurance sport; you're in it for the long haul. So you schedule a physical, check your blood pressure for free at the supermarket pharmacy, walk or jog, and hop on the treadmill that hides under the bed or doubles as a coat rack.

The length of your life, however, is really the short haul when compared to the long haul that is eternity. To prepare yourself for eternity requires conditioning that is spiritual rather than physical. Jesus prescribed a regimen so his followers could be in tip-top spiritual shape. It involves not just occasional exercise but a way of living every day that involves abiding faith, decency, witnessing, mercy, trust, and generosity.

If the Heels aren't ready when the opposition kicks off, they lose a game. If you aren't ready when Jesus calls, you lose eternity.

Proper conditioning is that fleeting moment between getting ready and going stale.

-- Alabama Coach Frank Thomas

Physical conditioning is good for the short run, but you also need to be in peak spiritual shape for the long haul.

DAY 61

ONE TOUGH COOKIE

Read 2 Corinthians 11:21b-29.

"Besides everything else, I face daily the pressure of my concern for all the churches" (v. 28).

Blood all over the place, a gory mess. And it's one of Coach Roy Williams' favorite photos.

Right next to pictures of his wife and children, Williams kept a shot that was right out of the most repulsive slasher flick, "a framed 8-by-10 of a young man drenched in his own blood." The frightful sight was Tyler Hansbrough, one of the greatest basketball players in North Carolina history, and Williams kept the photo to remind him of what *Sports Illustrated* called "the epic toughness of college basketball's fiercest gladiator."

The picture was snapped a half hour after a Duke player broke Hansbrough's nose with a flagrant foul during the 2006-07 season. "He has two cotton swabs up his nose and blood all over his arms and jersey, and he says, 'How do I look, Coach?'" said Williams, who still smiles at the memory. Hansbrough, in fact, sought out a photographer to have the picture taken. "I was like, 'Get a picture of this so people will believe how bloody it really was,'" he said. "It was gushing. It was crazy."

Hansbrough completed his All-American Carolina basketball career in 2009. He set a number of conference records, including most career points. Among others, he set school career records for most points and most rebounds. He is the only Tar Heel in history to be named unanimous first-team All-ACC all four seasons.

Sports Illustrated declared, "No player in memory has absorbed, initiated and (let's be honest) enjoyed more bumper-car moments in the lane" than Hansbrough. Williams' photo illustrates the truth of that statement as does an NCAA record Hansbrough set: most free throws made in a career.

You don't have to be a legendary UNC basketball player like Tyler Hansbrough to be tough. In America today, toughness isn't restricted to physical accomplishments and brute strength. Going to work every morning even when you feel bad, sticking by your rules for your children in a society that ridicules parental authority, making hard decisions about your aging parents' care often over their objections — you've got to be tough every day just to live honorably, decently, and justly.

Living faithfully requires toughness, too, though in America chances are you won't be imprisoned, stoned, or flogged this week for your faith as Paul was. Still, contemporary society exerts subtle, psychological, daily pressures on you to turn your back on your faith and your values. Popular culture promotes promiscuity, atheism, and gutter language; your children's schools have kicked God out; the corporate culture advocates amorality before the shrine of the almighty dollar.

You have to hang tough to keep the faith.

Winning isn't imperative, but getting tougher in the fourth quarter is.
— Bear Bryant

Life demands more than mere physical toughness;
you must be spiritually tough too.

DAY 62

IMPORTANT STUFF

Read Matthew 6:25-34.

"Seek first his kingdom and his righteousness, and all these things will be given to you as well" (v. 33).

The 'Virginia game' had become more than just a matter of football; it had become an impassioned vendetta."

The Tar Heels beat Virginia 17-0 in 1905 but then endured a string of losses that included the worst defeat in school history, 66-0 in 1912. Desperate for a win, administrators hired a new coach and allowed recruiting of players for the first time.

UNC's recruiting efforts were pretty feeble, though. One of those first recruits, Raby Tennent, recalled that the school didn't provide any scholarships or money, but instead offered something called "self-help." Tennent said, "This meant waiting on tables, marking tennis courts, . . . selling apples from back home from barrels. Board at the university was only $8.00 a month. So you can see the effort far outweighed the food."

From the moment he hit campus, Tennent was told, "Win the game with Virginia and nothing else mattered." The game was such a priority that for a while a player had to start against Virginia to letter.

After more losses to Virginia, Harvard All-American Thomas Campbell became the new coach in 1916. A crowd of 15,000 was on hand in Richmond on Nov. 30 for the season finale. Early in the second half, Bill Folger ripped off a 52-yard run for the game's only touchdown. George Tandy kicked the extra point, and UNC won 7-0.

Ecstatic fans carried the players around on their shoulders. For the first time in history, the school gave the athletes sweaters. Thomas Wolfe immortalized the UNC win by inserting a fictionalized account of it in his novel *The Web and the Rock*. In the book, Tennent was thinly disguised as Raby Bennett.

Beating Virginia may not be the most important thing in your life, but you do have priorities. What is it that you would surrender only with your dying breath? Your family? Every dime you have? Your Carolina season tickets?

What about God? Would you denounce your faith in Jesus Christ rather than lose your children? Or everything you own?

God doesn't force us to make such unspeakable choices; nevertheless, followers of Jesus Christ often become confused about their priorities because so much in our lives clamors for attention and time. It all seems so worthwhile and so deserving.

But Jesus' instructions are unequivocal: Seek God first. Turn to him first for help, fill your thoughts with what he wants for you and your life, use God's character as revealed in Jesus as the pattern for everything you do, and serve and obey him in all matters, at all moments. God – and God alone – is No. 1.

If you've ever heard me at a press conference, the first thing I do is give honor to God because he's first in my life.
-- College basketball coach Gary Waters

**God should be number one
in every area of our lives.**

DAY 63

DECIDE FOR YOURSELF

Read John 6:60-69.

"The words I have spoken to you are spirit and they are life. Yet there are some of you who do not believe" (vv. 63b-64a).

Talk about your basic no-brainer! You're a high school basketball coach and you're asked to join the staff of the University of North Carolina! For Roy Williams, though, the decision wasn't necessarily a slam dunk.

Williams' collegiate playing days ended after one season on the bench as a freshman at UNC in 1968-69. In 1973, he got his first hire as the head coach at Owen High School. During the summers Williams worked at UNC's basketball camp to pick up some extra cash and to network with other coaches. He was so reliable and so good with both the parents and the players that he was made the director of a gym at the start of his second season, a promotion that usually required several summers. When the NCAA allowed major programs to add a third assistant coach before the 1978-79 season, Dean Smith and assistant Bill Guthridge first thought of that "former freshman team player who was so effective at their summer camp." Smith offered him a job.

As improbable as it sounds, Williams hesitated. The problem was money. NCAA rules limited his salary to the equivalent of a full scholarship, less than $3,000 a year. Thus, "accepting the job at Carolina meant taking a pay cut and doing less than glamorous work," much of it administrative rather than coaching.

But he couldn't pass up this opportunity. To make extra money in those early days, Williams drove tapes of Smith's weekly television show across the state and sold team calendars.

Certainly, he never regretted the sacrifices required by the decision he made that charted the course of his life.

As with Roy Williams, the decisions you have made along the way have shaped your life at every pivotal moment. Some decisions you made suddenly and carelessly; some you made carefully and deliberately; some were forced upon you. You may have discovered that some of those spur-of-the-moment decisions have turned out better than your carefully considered ones.

Of all your life's decisions, however, none is more important than one you cannot ignore: What have you done with Jesus? Even in his time, people chose to follow Jesus or to reject him, and nothing has changed; the decision must still be made and nobody can make it for you. Ignoring Jesus won't work either; that is, in fact, a decision, and neither he nor the consequences of your decision will go away.

Carefully considered or spontaneous – how you arrive at a decision for Jesus doesn't matter; all that matters is that you get there.

If you make a decision that you think is the proper one at the time, then that's the correct decision.
-- *John Wooden*

A decision for Jesus may be spontaneous or considered; what counts is that you make it.

DAY 64

TRAGEDY

Read Job 1:1-2:10.

"In all this, Job did not sin by charging God with wrongdoing" (v. 1:22).

What should have been a time of great joy turned into the most tragic day of Steve Streater's life.

As a senior in 1980, Streater was first-team All-ACC as both a defensive back and a punter, the first player in ACC history to be named all-conference at two positions. Dick Crum's Heels went 11-1 and were ACC champions. In the 16-7 win over Texas in the Bluebonnet Bowl that year, Streater was the defensive MVP.

In April 1981, Streater was returning from Washington, D.C., where he had signed a contract to play for the Redskins, when a car accident left him paralyzed and confined to a wheelchair. Instead of giving up, Streater fought as he had fought on the football field and "was the same upbeat and positive guy" he had always been. He threw himself into physical therapy and eventually returned to Chapel Hill and earned his degree. He took care of and supported himself, driving a Porsche with special hand controls. He had not been wearing his seat belt that fateful day, and he helped persuade Carolina legislators to pass a seat-belt law. He also drove across the state to warn high-school students of the dangers of risky behavior.

When he became ill and was admitted to the hospital in 2009, the rumor circulated that Streater had finally given up. His brother, Eric, asked him if it were true; though he couldn't talk, Streater shook his head no. He died on June 19, 2009; he was 50. He had been scheduled to move out of the rehab center and into his own apartment in three days.

As one writer put it, Steve Streater "lived a full and positive life, the kind to be envied" despite the tragedy that struck him.

While we may receive it in varying degrees, suffering and tragedy are par for life's course. What we do with tragedy when it strikes us – as Steve Streater's story illustrates – determines to a great extent how we live the rest of our lives.

We can – in accordance with the bitter suggestion Job's wife offered -- "Curse God and die," or we can trust God and live. That is, we can plunge into endless despair or we can lean upon the power of a transcendent faith in an almighty God who offers us hope in our darkest hours.

We don't have to understand tragedy; we certainly don't have to like it or believe there's anything fair about it. What we must do in such times, however, is trust in God's all-powerful love for us and his promise that all things will work for good for those who love him.

In choosing a life of ongoing trust in God in the face of our suffering, we prevent the greatest tragedy of all: that of a soul being cast into hell.

Steve [Streater] lived life like we always think we should.
-- Eric Streater

Tragedy can drive us into despair and death
or into the life-sustaining arms of almighty God.

DAY 65

THE BEAUTIFUL PEOPLE

Read Matthew 23:23-28.

"Woe to you, teachers of the law and Pharisees, you hypocrites! You are like whitewashed tombs, which look beautiful on the outside, but on the inside are full of dead men's bones and everything unclean" (v. 27).

When you hit the hardwood for the Heels, it's all about how you play. Except maybe in Dante Calabria's case. He drew almost as much interest for how he looked as how he played.

Not one to hand out compliments freely, Dean Smith once characterized Calabria as "an exceptional basketball player who probably won't get his due except from other coaches." Calabria helped the Heels win the national championship in 1993 as a freshman and played on two more Final Four teams, averaging 12 points per game as a senior in 1996. He was so versatile that he played four different positions on that '96 squad.

He was a fan favorite and not just for how well he played. He was, in fact, what one sportswriter characterized as a "glamour guy," whose appearance drew a lot of attention. He got so many calls from women that he finally had to get an unlisted number. "I guess some people have nothing better to do with their lives," Calabria said.

Much of the interest, though, centered around Calabria's haircut, "which typically had Smith Center denizens wondering what in the name of Agassi was next." The dos included "a slick-backed

Godfather look, [a] Prince Valiant cut, an Elvis sideburns incarnation, the ill-fated buzzed sidewall effort and a McCartney bob," the latter the style with which he ended his Carolina career.

The Georgia Tech mascot noticed Calabria's sense of style, showing up for a game with a container labeled "Calabria's Hair Gel for Women." The container was a 25-gallon garbage can.

Dante Calabria was one of UNC's beautiful people.

Remember the brunette who sat behind you in history class? Or the blonde in English? And how about that hunk from the next apartment who washes his car every Saturday morning and just forces you to get outside earlier than you really want to?

We do love those beautiful people.

It is worth remembering amid our adulation of superficial beauty that *Vogue* or *People* probably wouldn't have been too enamored of Jesus' looks. Isaiah 53 declares that our savior "had no beauty or majesty to attract us to him, nothing in his appearance that we should desire him."

Though Jesus never urged folks to walk around with body odor and unwashed hair, he did admonish us to avoid being overly concerned with physical beauty, which fades with age despite tucks and Botox. What matters to God is inner beauty, which reveals itself in the practice of justice, mercy, and faith, and which is not only lifelong but eternal.

[Dante] Calabria looks more Hollywood than hardwood.
                                        -- Sportswriter Steve Elling

**When it comes to looking good to God,
it's what's inside that counts.**

DAY 66

WATERBORNE

Read Acts 10:34-48.

"Can anyone keep these people from being baptized with water? They have received the Holy Spirit just as we have" (v. 47).

Charlotte Smith made Van Hatchell's wish come true -- as well as that of Tar Heel fans everywhere.

Van, son of UNC women's basketball coach Sylvia Hatchell, was five years old in April 1994 when his mama's team traveled to Richmond for the Final Four. He spotted a wishing well at the team's hotel, tossed a nickel and a penny into the water, closed his eyes, and wished that his mother's team would win the school's first women's basketball national championship.

That title seemed lost when Louisiana Tech led 59-57 and a Heel shot went awry with four seconds left to play. A mad scramble ensued until Marion Jones tied up a Tech player for a jump ball with only 0.7 seconds left. At first, the possession arrow pointed Tech's way, but then officials switched it. UNC had the ball.

On the inbounds pass, junior Stephanie Lawrence spotted Smith coming off a screen by Sylvia Crawley and hit her with a perfect pass. Smith immediately hoisted the game-winning three-point shot. "I knew as soon as the ball left Charlotte's hands that it was going in," Hatchell said. "I couldn't even watch it," Smith said. "I just thank God for helping it come through." Smith was promptly buried at midcourt beneath her jubilant – and national champion – teammates.

About that water back at the hotel. After he made his wish but before the game, Van discovered that someone had cleaned the fountain of its coins; he was sure his wish wouldn't come true now. His father, Sammy, explained that his wish would still come true "because the wishes wash off into the water."

So the real source of the miracle championship lay in the water.

Children's wading pools and swimming pools in the backyard. Fishing, boating, skiing, and swimming at a lake. Sun, sand, and surf at the beach. If there's any water around, we'll probably be in it, on it, or near it. If there's not any at hand, we'll build a dam and create our own.

We love the wet stuff for its recreational uses, but water first and foremost is about its absolute necessity to support and maintain life. From its earliest days, the Christian church appropriated water as an image of life through the ritual of baptism. Since the time of the arrival of the Holy Spirit at Pentecost, baptism with water has been the symbol of entry into the Christian community. It is water that marks a person as belonging to Jesus. It is through water that a person proclaims that Jesus is his Lord.

There's something in the water, all right. There is life.

Swimmers are like teabags; you don't know how strong they are until you put them in the water.
– Source unknown

There is life in the water:
physical life and spiritual life.

DAY 67

GOOD SPORTS

Read Titus 2:1-8.

"Show integrity, seriousness and soundness of speech that cannot be condemned, so that those who oppose you may be ashamed because they have nothing bad to say about us" (vv. 7b, 8).

An act of sportsmanship led to one of the sloppiest game of the storied UNC-Duke rivalry.

Dubbed by sportswriters "The Wild Bunch," the Tar Heels of 1970-71 were totally dismissed by the preseason prognosticators. With a lineup including Steve Previs, George Karl, Lee Dedmon, Bill Chamberlin, and Dennis Wuycik (first-team All-ACC that season), they upset second-ranked South Carolina in January and romped to the ACC title with a 12-2 record on their way to a 26-win season. They lost to South Carolina 52-51 in the tournament, though, and thus were relegated to the NIT. So was Duke.

Fretting that his players would get rusty practicing against each other, Duke coach Bucky Waters called up Dean Smith with an unusual request. He asked if he could bring his team to Chapel Hill to work out with the Tar Heels. When the league office didn't object, the unusual practice was on.

"Duke and Carolina players who considered themselves arch enemies got acquainted, and several formed lifelong friendships from their afternoon together." They conducted a serious practice, running offensive and defensive sets against each other.

TAR HEELS

They wound up playing each other in the NIT semifinals. As a result of the practice, each team knew what the other was doing, and not surprisingly the game was sloppy, marked by poor shooting and too many turnovers. When one team called a play, the other was in perfect defensive position. "What took you so long to get here" was a comment heard regularly on the court.

The Tar Heels won 73-67 in an ugly game that resulted from a beautiful afternoon of sportsmanship.

One of life's paradoxes is that many who would never consider cheating on the tennis court or the racquetball court to gain an advantage think nothing of doing so in other areas of their life. In other words, the good sportsmanship they practice on the golf course or the Monopoly board doesn't carry over. They play with the truth, cut corners, abuse others verbally, run roughshod over the weaker, and generally cheat whenever they can to gain an advantage on the job or in their personal relationships.

But good sportsmanship is a way of living, not just of playing. Shouldn't you accept defeat without complaint (You don't have to like it.); win gracefully without gloating; treat your competition with fairness, courtesy, generosity, and respect? That's the way one team treats another in the name of sportsmanship. That's the way one person treats another in the name of Jesus.

One person practicing sportsmanship is better than a hundred teaching it.
                                                        -- Knute Rockne

**Sportsmanship -- treating others with courtesy,
fairness, and respect -- is a way of living,
not just a way of playing.**

DAY 68

FAMILY TIES

Read Mark 3:31-35.

"[Jesus] said, 'Here are my mother and my brothers! Whoever does God's will is my brother and sister and mother'" (vv. 34-35).

It was about as big as a family argument could get." The occasion for this squabble was what was called "an unprecedented bowl matchup."

Bill Dooley's Tar Heels of 1971 went 9-2 and won the first of back-to-back ACC championships. A 7-3 squeaker against Wake Forest was the only conference game that was even close. The reward for the championship season was a trip to the Gator Bowl where UNC would meet the University of Georgia – coached by Bill Dooley's brother, Vince.

The media hopped all over the fraternal aspect of the game, calling it "one of the most emotionally devastating matchups in college football." The game was also a rather strange encounter because the teams were so much alike. The head Heel had come to Chapel Hill from Athens where he had been an assistant to his brother; as a result, the teams had styles that were "strikingly similar . . . down to the warmup drills." "Our two offenses were practically identical," Bill Dooley said. His brother "even had my old offensive line coach, Jimmy Vickers, on his staff."

The game was close throughout with the two squads winding up with the same number of rushing plays: 51. Late in the third quarter, Ken Craven kicked a field goal for a 3-0 Carolina lead, but UGA later scored for a 7-3 win.

"We never thought that we would be competing against each other," Bill Dooley said about the contest against his brother, "because football schedules are made 10 years in advance, and our schools were not even scheduled. All of a sudden here we are in a bowl game, and you have to get ready to play against your brother's team."

Some wit said families are like fudge, mostly sweet with a few nuts. You can probably call the names of your sweetest relatives, whom you cherish, and of the nutty ones too, whom you mostly try to avoid at a family reunion.

Like it or not, you have a family, and that's God's doing. God cherishes the family so much that he chose to live in one as a son, a brother, and a cousin.

One of Jesus' more startling actions was to redefine the family. No longer is it a single household of blood relatives or even a clan or a tribe. Jesus' family is the result not of an accident of birth but rather a conscious choice. All those who do God's will are members of Jesus' family.

What a startling and wonderful thought! You have family members out there you don't even know who stand ready to love you just because you're part of God's family.

It was almost like playing against yourself.
-- UGA defensive end Chuck Heard on the 1971 Gator Bowl

For followers of Jesus, family comes not from
a shared ancestry but from a shared faith.

DAY 69

IN SO MANY WORDS

Read Matthew 12:33-37.

"For out of the overflow of the heart the mouth speaks. The good man brings good things out of the good stored up in him, and the evil man brings evil things out of the evil stored up in him" (vv. 34b-35).

She has a gift for gab. She is never at a loss for words."

So spoke UNC softball coach Donna Papa about one of her players in 1997. That player couldn't help it, though; she came by her propensity for chatter quite naturally. Her grandfather was Yogi Berra.

Lindsay Berra lettered as a freshman for the Carolina softball team in 1996 after coming south from New Jersey without an athletic scholarship. She battled for playing time as a leftfielder and was also the lone woman in a men's recreational ice hockey league. She was certainly her own individual.

But she was widely known as "Yogi Berra's granddaughter," a connection about which she was quite proud. And so was Yogi, who took no credit for her abilities. "She did it on her own," he said. "She's a good little hustler who puts everything into it." "To me, he's Grandpa," Lindsay said. "When I meet somebody, I just say: 'I'm Lindsay.' I let them figure it out." Yogi didn't think too much of his granddaughter's playing hockey, though. "I tell her she's crazy [to play that game]," he said, "but she loves it."

Lindsay once elaborated on the legend behind her grandfa-

TAR HEELS

ther's reputation for delivering humorous, mind-twisting quotes. Yogi and she once "sat down and went through each one [of the quotes] in a book," she said. "He said about 50 percent of them."

While Lindsay didn't "toss out as many quotable quips as her grandpa, the bloodline [was] obvious." For instance, once when Papa was giving her a few batting tips, she blurted out, "I can't think and hit at the same time!"

Her grandfather would have been proud.

These days, everybody's got something to say and likely as not a place to say it. Talk radio, 24-hour sports and news TV channels, *Oprah, The View*. Talk has really become cheap.

But words still have power, and that includes not just those of the talking heads, hucksters, and pundits on television, but ours also. Our words are perhaps the most powerful force we possess for good or for bad. The words we speak today can belittle, wound, humiliate, and destroy. They can also inspire, heal, protect, and create. Our words both shape and define us. They also reveal to the world the depth of our faith.

We should never make the mistake of underestimating the power of the spoken word. After all, speaking the Word was the only means Jesus had to get his message across – and look what he managed to do.

We must always watch what we say, because others sure will.

My daddy always taught me these words: care and share.
— *Tiger Woods*

Choose your words carefully; they are the most powerful force you have for good or for bad.

DAY 70

EXCUSES, EXCUSES

Read Luke 9:57-62.

"Another said, 'I will follow you, Lord; but first let me go back and say good-by to my family'" (v. 61).

Duke once had an original excuse for losing to UNC: The Blue Devils blamed the loss on the Tar Heel student manager.

During the unbeaten national championship season of 1956-57, the 17-0 Heels hosted Duke on Feb. 9. The decision was made to broadcast the clash over local public TV, the first basketball game of any kind on television. The process was called "Broadvision." It didn't have audio, so fans had to watch the game on their black-and-white TV's and listen to Ray Reeve's play-by-play on radio.

UNC Comptroller Billy Carmichael, Jr. and Bill Friday, the president of the state's Consolidated University system, were the brains behind the idea, correctly foreseeing that college basketball could be a success on TV. Hours before the game, they "were using hammers and picks to chisel a hole in the cinderblock wall behind the bleachers in Woollen Gym so they could fit the lens of the Broadvision camera."

Curious viewers in Raleigh, Greensboro, and Charlotte saw a thriller with a curious ending. Carolina lost an eight-point lead in the final two minutes. As the Duke guard who had tied the game hurried back on defense, he glanced over to the hand-operated wooden scoreboard at the corner of the Carolina bench. It read "UNC 73 Duke 71." Believing his team was behind with only a few seconds left, he intentionally fouled Tommy Kearns.

But the Carolina student manager had been so caught up in the excitement that he hadn't flipped over the "two" and the "three" under VISITORS. The electronic scoreboard reflected the correct score, but that was not the score the Duke guard saw. Kearns sank both free throws for the 75-73 Carolina win.

Afterward, Duke was ready with an excuse: The scorekeeper "cost us the game. They didn't beat us. Their scorekeeper did."

Has some of your most creative thinking involved excuses for not going in to work? Have you discovered that an unintended benefit of computers is that you can always blame them for the destruction of all your hard work? Don't you manage to stammer or stutter some justification when a state trooper pulls you over? We're usually pretty good at making excuses to cover our failures or to get out of something we don't particularly want to do.

That holds true for our faith life also. The Bible is too hard to understand so I won't read it; the weather's too pretty to be shut up in church; praying in public is embarrassing and I'm not very good at it anyway. The plain truth is, though, that whatever excuses we make for not following Jesus wholeheartedly are not good enough.

Jesus made no excuses to avoid dying for us; we should offer none to avoid living for him.

There are a thousand reasons for failure but not a single excuse.
-- Former NFL player Mike Reid

Try though we might, no excuses can justify
our failure to follow Jesus wholeheartedly.

DAY 71

IN THE KNOW

Read John 4:19-26, 39-42.

"They said to the woman, . . . 'Now we have heard for ourselves, and we know that this man really is the Savior of the world'" (v. 42).

I just knew we could do it." So spoke North Carolina quarterback Junior Edge. Turned out he was right.

The Tar Heels of 1963 went 8-2 in the regular season, won the school's first ACC championship, and then trounced Air Force 35-0 in the Gator Bowl. The team set a new school standard for total offensive yardage, breaking the record established by the storied Charlie Justice-Art Weiner team of 1948.

The bowl game may well have been decided by where the two teams stayed. Newspaperman Bob Quincy noted that UNC was "housed in a plush hotel and had great accommodations and food. The Carolina team perhaps had the best rooming situation anyone ever did." The boys from the Academy, however, were housed in an Army base near Orlando where, Quincy said, "they didn't have a Christmas vacation . . . and they were being treated like GIs. . . . Had the Air Force kids had first-class accommodations, they might have been in a better frame of mind to play football."

The Heels had only one bad showing all season, a loss to Michigan State; the second loss was 11-7 to Clemson. The finale against Duke, though, was a thriller that came down to the last Tar Heel possession and their quarterback's confidence.

TAR HEELS

UNC jumped out to a 13-0 on touchdowns by Ken Willard, who won the league rushing title that season with 648 yards, and Eddie Kessler. But Duke rallied to lead 14-13 with less than two minutes left. Edge wasn't worried. "I had confidence all along," he said. He told his teammates, "Boys, we've got more than a minute and 20 seconds. We can do a lot of scoring in that time."

They did just enough. With 33 seconds remaining, Max Chapman kicked a field goal for a 16-14 UNC win.

Junior Edge knew North Carolina would win in the same way you know certain things in your life. That your spouse loves you, for instance. That you are good at your job. That tea should be iced and sweetened. That a bad day fishing is still better than a good day at work. That the best barbecue comes from a pig. You know these things even though no mathematician or philosopher can prove any of this on paper.

It's the same way with faith in Jesus: You just know that he is God's son and the savior of the world. You know it in the same way that you know the University of North Carolina is the only team worth pulling for: with every fiber of your being, with all your heart, your mind, and your soul.

You just know, and because you know him, Jesus knows you. And that is all you really need to know.

You know you're getting old when you start watching golf on TV and enjoying it.
-- Comedian Larry Miller

**A life of faith is lived in certainty and conviction:
You just know you know.**

DAY 72

THE COMEBACK KIDS

Read Acts 9:1-22.

*"All those who heard him were astonished and asked,
'Isn't he the man who raised havoc in Jerusalem among
those who call on this name?'" (v. 21)*

Let's do the things we practiced, and we can still win." What followed that declaration was what may well be the most incredible comeback in college basketball history.

On March 2, 1974, in the regular season finale, UNC trailed Duke 86-78 with only seventeen seconds left when Dean Smith uttered his improbable pronouncement about still winning. Bobby Jones was at the line for two, but all Duke had to do to win was make one successful inbounds pass. Smith ordered a trapping defense after the free throws with a time out immediately after they stole the pass and scored. Jones made both shots, Duke flubbed the inbounds pass, and John Kuester laid it in for two. Time out. 86-82 with thirteen seconds left.

The whole scenario incredibly repeated itself. Duke fumbled the inbounds pass, and UNC actually missed two shots before Jones' put-back made it a two-point game with six seconds left to play. The thousands of fans who had headed for the exits began scrambling back to their seats.

Duke finally managed a successful inbounds pass, and UNC fouled immediately. One-and-one with four seconds left. The shot hit back rim, and Ed Stahl grabbed the rebound. Final UNC time out with three seconds left.

In the huddle, Smith again told his players to do what they did in practice. They did. Sophomore center Mitch Kupchak hit Walter Davis with a long pass. Davis dribbled twice and launched a 28-footer that slammed off the backboard through the hoop.

Carmichael Auditorium erupted into bedlam; the fans stormed the court, leading Smith to exclaim, "I thought the game was tied." In the age before the three-point shot, it was, and UNC completed the incredible comeback by winning 96-92 in overtime.

Life will have its setbacks whether they result from personal failures or from forces and people beyond your control. Being a Christian and a faithful follower of Jesus Christ doesn't insulate you from getting into deep trouble. Maybe financial problems suffocated you. A serious illness sidelined you. Or your family was hit with a great tragedy. Life is a series of victories and defeats. Winning isn't about avoiding defeat; it's about getting back up to compete again. It's about making a comeback of your own.

When you avail yourself of God's grace and God's power, your comeback is always greater than your setback. You are never too far behind, and it's never too late in life's game for Jesus to lead you to victory, to turn trouble into triumph. As it was with the Heels in that 1974 game against Duke and with Paul, it's not how you start that counts; it's how you finish.

Wouldn't it be fun to catch up after being so far behind?
-- Dean Smith to his players during the last time out against Duke

**In life, victory is truly a matter of how you finish
and whether you finish with Jesus at your side.**

DAY 73

A HOLLYWOOD ENDING

Read Luke 24:1-12.

"Why do you look for the living among the dead? He is not here; he has risen!" (vv. 5, 6a)

Hollywood wouldn't touch it: Running back doesn't get to play much in college but then goes on to become a pro football star. It's just too corny and unbelievable -- but it's the true story of Willie Parker.

Parker never won the starting job at UNC on some teams that weren't very good. He had his most success at Chapel Hill his freshman season of 2000 when he rushed for 355 yards on 84 carries, but under the new regime of head coach John Bunting in 2001, "Parker got a bit lost in the running back shuffle." He started five games total in his sophomore and junior seasons and three more games his senior year when he rushed for 181 yards on 48 carries.

Not surprisingly, Parker wasn't drafted by the pros in 2004, so his football career was over, right? Hey, this is Hollywood.

Enter Dan Rooney, Jr., son of the owner of the Pittsburgh Steelers, who had seen Parker play and who recommended the team sign him as a free agent. He made the roster and rode the bench until the season finale when he ran for 102 yards in three quarters.

Early in 2005, Parker became the starter and the second undrafted back in NFL history to rush for more than 1,200 yards.

In the Super Bowl following the season, Parker had a 75-yard touchdown run, the longest in Super Bowl history at the time. He was All-Pro in both 2006 and 2007 and the team's MVP in 2006.

Only the most befuddled Tinseltown screen writer could come up with such a far-fetched story, and any self-respecting producer wouldn't touch it. But it's Willie Parker's real-life Hollywood ending.

The world tells us that happy endings are for fairy tales and the movies, that reality is Cinderella dying in childbirth and her prince getting killed in a peasant uprising. But that's just another of the world's lies.

The truth is that Jesus Christ has been producing happy endings for almost two millennia. That's because in Jesus lies the power to change and to rescue a life no matter how desperate the situation. Jesus is the master at putting shattered lives back together, of healing broken hearts and broken relationships, of resurrecting lost dreams.

And as for living happily ever after – God really means it. The greatest Hollywood ending of them all was written on a Sunday morning centuries ago when Jesus left a tomb and death behind. With faith in Jesus, your life can have that same ending. You live with God in peace, joy, and love – forever.

The End.

If I had it to do all over again, I'd still go to North Carolina.
-- Willie Parker

Hollywood's happy endings are products
of imagination; the happy endings Jesus produces
are real and are yours for the asking.

DAY 74

TIME FOR A CHANGE

Read Romans 6:1-14.

"Just as Christ was raised from the dead through the glory of the Father, we too may live a new life" (v. 4).

The Heels just wanted to win the game. They didn't know they were changing all of college basketball.

On March 7, 1982, the top-ranked Tar Heels met No. 3 Virginia in the finals of the ACC Tournament. With 7:30 to go in the game and UNC leading 44-43, Dean Smith gave point guard Jimmy Black the signal to go into the Four Corners offense. Surprisingly, Virginia countered by doing nothing. A stalemate ensued with the Heels passing the ball around on the outside for six minutes while many fans booed or chanted "BOR-ING!"

With only 28 seconds left, Virginia fouled Matt Doherty, and he sank a free throw, one of only seven attempted the entire game, the tournament record for fewest free throws. With three seconds left, he hit another pair and Virginia got a meaningless dunk at the buzzer. UNC won 47-45 by scoring 13 points in the last half to Virginia's 14.

Reaction to the game was universally vitriolic. One writer said Smith's decision created "a monster of a controversy." Longtime Tar Heel announcer Woody Durham said the game "had an incredible impact on the sport" as it "galvanized opposition to the slowdown."

Only two months later, the ACC voted to experiment with a

TAR HEELS

30-second shot clock and a 19-foot three-point line. Within a few seasons, both became fixtures of the college game.

"Our game at Virginia was a watershed," Black later wrote, "but we didn't think of it that way." "I don't care if the score had been 2-0, it would have been a great win," Michael Jordan said.

The Heels changed the college game, but nothing could change the win that day and the national championship they won three weeks later.

Anyone who asserts no change is needed in his or her life isn't paying attention. Every life has doubt, worry, fear, failure, frustration, unfulfilled dreams, and unsuccessful relationships in some combination. The memory and consequences of our past often haunt and trouble us.

Recognizing the need for change in our lives, though, doesn't mean the changes that will bring about hope, joy, peace, and fulfillment will occur. We need some power greater than ourselves or we wouldn't be where we are.

So where can we turn? Where lies the hope for a changed life? It lies in an encounter with he who is the Lord of all Hope: Jesus Christ. For a life turned over to Jesus, change is inevitable. With Jesus in charge, the old self with its painful and destructive ways of thinking, feeling, loving, and living is transformed.

A changed life is always only a talk with Jesus away.

Change is an essential element of sports, as it is of life.
-- Erik Brady, USA Today

**In Jesus lie the hope and the power
that change lives.**

DAY 75

CONFIDENCE MAN

Read Micah 7:5-7.

"As for me, I will look to the Lord, I will wait for the God of my salvation" (v. 7 NRSV).

Deems May lost his confidence – which turned out to be the best thing for his football career.

May arrived in Chapel Hill in 1987 as the "next new great hope as a Tar Heel quarterback." Highly recruited, he had begun getting letters from college coaches as an eighth grader. He apparently lived up to the high expectations when he started at Carolina as a redshirt freshman in Mack Brown's first game as head coach. South Carolina blasted the Heels 31-10. The next week the Oklahoma Sooners came to town and handed UNC "one of the most one-sided 28-0 decisions in football history. May's career as a quarterback essentially was over."

"I never really had a chance, but that wasn't anybody's fault," May said from the perspective as a fifth-year senior. "I just wasn't ready." May admitted he may have been overrated as a quarterback and that he was set back by missing most of his senior season in high school because of injuries.

But May also admitted to something worse for a quarterback than all these factors. "I lost confidence in myself and that was it," he said. "It didn't make any difference after that if I could have been a good quarterback or not."

The following spring May was moved to tight end. "I was

ready to move," he said. "I'd never considered myself anything but a quarterback, but I was ready to try something else. I just wanted to play."

He won the starting job as a junior in 1990 and played his senior season at 6'5", 245 pounds, size that drew the attention of pro scouts. He was drafted by the San Diego Chargers and played eight seasons in the NFL – quite confidently.

You need confidence in all areas of your life. You're confident the company you work for will pay you on time, or you wouldn't go to work. You turn the ignition confident your car will start. When you flip a switch, you expect the light to come on.

Confidence in other people and in things is often misplaced, though. Companies go broke; car batteries die; light bulbs burn out. Even the people you love the most sometimes let you down.

So where can you place your trust with absolute confidence you won't be betrayed? In the promises of God.

Such confidence is easy, of course, when everything's going your way, but what about when you cry as Micah did, "What misery is mine!" As Micah declares, that's when your confidence in God must be its strongest. That's when you wait for the Lord confident that God will not fail you, that he will never let you down.

When it gets right down to the wood-chopping, the key to winning is confidence.

-- *Darrell Royal*

**People, things, and organizations
will let you down; only God can be trusted
absolutely and confidently.**

DAY 76

HOME SWEET HOME

Read Joshua 24:14-27.

"Choose for yourselves this day whom you will serve. . . .
But as for me and my household, we will serve the Lord"
(v. 15).

It's just a fact: When the Heels play at home, they win.

The Dean Smith Student Activities Center -- or as it is more familiarly known, the Dean Dome -- opened in 1986 as the third-largest on-campus arena in the country. The privately funded palace included among its amenities individual mirrored vanities for the players. Asked what he liked best about the place, senior guard Steve Hale replied, "The shower heads are so high."

The Dome was baptized on January 18, 1986, opening just in time for a truly titanic contest. Workmen were still sawing, hammering, and painting everything in sight Carolina Blue when Smith held a rehearsal scrimmage before about 5,000 students to get a feel for how noisy the place would be. Fittingly, the opponent for that special night was Duke. The two teams were a combined 33-0, but that probably didn't really matter. As Duke forward David Henderson said, "If it's Duke-Carolina, it's the most intense rivalry of all time."

The night belonged to Hale, who had 28 points, five assists, four rebounds, and three steals in 31 minutes of fervid play. Hale spent the night conducting backdoor forays that netted him open short-range shots, which led him to say, "I don't feel like I had such a great day. Anybody can make layups."

Oh, yes. The Tar Heels won 95-92, which was only appropriate since they have pretty much done nothing but win ever since in what has been called "one of the most formidable home-court advantages in the country." After the 2008-09 season, the Heels were 285-52 in the Dome, a staggering .846 percentage.

The Dean Dome provides such a home-court advantage for UNC that it's like having a sixth man on the floor.

You enter your home to find love, security, and joy. It's the place where your heart feels warmest, your laughter comes easiest, and your life is its richest. It is the center of and the reason for everything you do and everything you are.

How can a home be such a place?

If it is a home where grace is spoken before every meal, it is such a place. If it is a home where the Bible is read, studied, and discussed by the whole family gathered together, it is such a place. If it is a home that serves as a jumping-off point for the whole family to go to church, not just on Sunday morning and not just occasionally, but regularly, it is such a place. If it is a home where the name of God is spoken with reverence and awe and not with disrespect and indifference, it is such a place.

In other words, a house becomes a true home when God is part of the family.

This is one heck of a home-court advantage.
-- Connecticut Coach Jim Calhoun on the Dean Dome

A home is full when all the family members –
including God -- are present.

NOT WHAT THEY SEEM

Read Habakkuk 1:2-11.

"Why do you make me look at injustice? Why do you tolerate wrong? Destruction and violence are before me; there is strife, and conflict abounds" (v. 3).

At first glance, Chris Webber's call of a timeout he didn't have in the closing seconds of the 1993 national championship game seems like Tar Heel luck. Closer scrutiny, however, reveals that just maybe it wasn't what it seemed.

Unmistakably, the Heels have been the beneficiaries of perhaps the two most famous gaffes in NCAA finals history. In 1982 with five seconds left, Georgetown's Fred Brown inexplicably found James Worthy wide open and hit him with a perfect pass, also throwing a freshman named Michael Jordan into what would become his accustomed role of hardcourt hero.

Then, in 1993, the Heels led Michigan only 73-71 with 20 seconds left when Webber rebounded a missed Carolina free throw. Forgotten in the hubbub surrounding the timeout call was that Webber clearly dragged his pivot foot before he started dribbling, and the officials had a momentary lapse of reason and eyesight and didn't make the obvious traveling call.

Webber made up for the refs' mistake, though. Senior forward George Lynch and junior guard Derrick Phelps trapped Webber, who covered up with 11 seconds left and signaled for the fateful timeout. Donald Williams, the MVP of the Final Four, hit both technical free throws and then two more after Michigan fouled on the ensuing possession. The Heels were national champions.

Luck? Deja voodoo in New Orleans? It sure seemed like it. Maybe not, though.

Early in the second half, the Tar Heels made a play that seemed meaningless at the time. Playing ferocious defense, Phelps and Lynch denied Michigan a simple inbounds pass. To avoid a five-second call, Wolverine Juwan Howard had to burn a timeout, the one Webber didn't have at game's end.

Sometimes in life – just as in basketball -- things aren't what they seem. In our violent and convulsive times, we must confront the possibility of a new reality: that we are helpless in the face of anarchy; that injustice, destruction, and violence are pandemic in and symptomatic of our modern age. It seems that anarchy is winning, that the system of standards, values, and institutions we have cherished is crumbling while we watch.

But we should not be deceived or disheartened. God is in fact the arch-enemy of chaos, the creator of order and goodness and the architect of all of history. God is in control. We often misinterpret history as the record of mankind's accomplishments -- which it isn't -- rather than the unfolding of God's plan -- which it is. That plan has a clearly defined end: God will make everything right. In that day things will be what they seem.

Lucky, yes. Fortunate, yes. But we're still NCAA champs.
-- Dean Smith after the win over Michigan in 1993

**The forces of good and decency often seem
helpless before evil's power, but don't be fooled:
God is in control and will set things right.**

DAY 78

WEATHERPROOFED

Read Nahum 1:3-9.

"His way is in the whirlwind and the storm, and clouds are the dust of his feet" (v. 3b).

It was the most exciting game nobody saw.

Dick Crum's Tar Heels of 1981 went 10-2, ending the season with a thrilling 31-27 win over Arkansas in the Gator Bowl on Dec. 28. The first half was played under typical Florida conditions, clear but humid, and ended in a 10-10 tie, but everything changed during halftime. "When we came out of the tunnel from halftime," remembered UNC quarterback Rod Elkins, "you could see the fog start to roll in. And it just kept coming."

By the middle of the third quarter, the fog rolling across the Gator Bowl from the St. John's River was so thick folks in the stands couldn't see anything. The fans watching the game at home on television didn't fare much better. They all missed an exciting last half. Elkins led three straight touchdown drives to propel Carolina to a 31-10 lead with 7:29 left in the game. Ethan Horton scored from the one, Elkins sneaked in from the one, and Horton got in from the four.

The fog didn't make it easy. Quarterbacks coach Cleve Bryant remembered that the Heels "had installed some pretty nifty hand signals for that game because when Coach [Lou] Holtz [the Arkansas head coach] was at N.C. State he tried to steal our plays." When the fog rolled in, though, Elkins couldn't see Bryant's signals. So Bryant "would run onto the field, tell Rod the play, and run right off. Probably broke every rule there is by doing that."

Arkansas rallied ferociously with two late touchdowns and a safety and had the ball with less than a minute to play. Freshman Ronnie Snipes, who had played for only two snaps in the game, sacked the Hog quarterback to seal the win.

But, of course, nobody saw it.

A thunderstorm washes away your golf game or the picnic with the kids. Lightning knocks out the electricity just as you settle in at the computer. A tornado interrupts your Sunday dinner and sends everyone scurrying to the hallway. A hurricane cancels your beach trip.

For all our technology and our knowledge, we are still at the mercy of the weather, able only to get a little more advance warning than in the past. The weather answers only to God. Rain and hail will fall where they want to; fog will be totally inconsiderate of something as important as a Tar Heel football game.

We stand mute before the awesome power of the weather, but we should be even more awestruck at the power of the one who controls it, a power beyond our imagining. Neither, however, can we imagine the depths of God's love for us, a love that drove him to die on a cross for us.

We played a good game, we beat a good team, but all anyone talks about is the fog.

-- *UNC quarterback Rod Elkins*

**Almighty God's power is beyond anything
we can imagine, but so is his love for us.**

DAY 79

HOW YOU SEE IT

Read John 20:11-18.

"Mary stood outside the tomb crying" (v. 11).

Carolina was "in slow decline with an aging coach while Duke boasted hot new stars of the MTV era." Correct or not, many had this perspective upon the bitter rivals as the 1988-89 basketball season began.

Clearly, by this time, both Duke and North Carolina were "considered colossal basketball vessels sailing the same waters." The problem for the Heels, though, was that the two programs were also seen by many as "big ships passing in the night." While both schools had won two ACC tournaments and reached the Final Four twice in the 1980s, Carolina's success had occurred back in 1981 and '82. Duke's titles were in 1986 and '88.

What the Tar Heel basketball program needed was a big win over the Blue Devils.

On Jan. 18, 1989, the Heels traveled to Durham with their season threatening to unravel. They had lost two of their last three, including a 23-point whipping by Virginia. Moreover, Jeff Lebo, the Heels' star senior guard, was sidelined by a sprained ankle. Duke, on the other hand, was 13-0 and ranked No. 1.

Dean Smith, however, knew what it would take for his team to win: He needed a great game from King Rice and rebounding from J.R. Reid and Scott Williams. They would make up for Lebo's absence by committee.

TAR HEELS

As Art Chansky put it, "Ironically, it may have been Lebo's injury that helped Carolina the most on this night." Rice had good penetration skills and he used them as the Devils refused to pull in tight on defense. As a team, the Heels outrebounded Duke by seventeen.

North Carolina broke open a close game late and won easily 91-71. Perspectives underwent an immediate adjustment.

Your perspective goes a long way toward determining whether you slink through life amid despair, anger, and hopelessness or stride boldly through life with joy and hope. Mary is a good example. On that first Easter morning, she stood by Jesus' tomb crying, her heart broken, because she still viewed everything through the perspective of Jesus' death. But how her attitude, her heart, and her life changed when she saw the morning through the perspective of Jesus' resurrection.

So it is with life and death for all of us. You can't avoid death, but you can determine how you perceive it. Is it fearful, dark, fraught with peril and uncertainty? Or is it a simple little passageway to glory, the light, and loved ones, an elevator ride to paradise?

It's a matter of perspective that depends totally on whether or not you're standing by Jesus' side when it arrives.

For some people it's the end of the rainbow, but for us it's the end of the finish line.

— Rower Larisa Healy

Whether death is your worst enemy or a solicitous chauffeur is a matter of perspective.

DAY 80

A LONG SHOT

Read Matthew 9:9-13.

"[Jesus] saw a man named Matthew sitting at the tax collector's booth. 'Follow me,' he told him, and Matthew got up and followed him" (v. 9).

Irv Holdash knew the truth: He was a long shot to make the North Carolina football team.

When Holdash came to Chapel Hill in 1946, he joined a team flush with talented, experienced former servicemen. End Ken Powell, a 1949 All-America, had to fight his way through fifty ends to make the team. One player who was All-Southern in 1945 fell to fifth string in 1946 when the veterans returned. North Carolina had so many talented players that Wake Forest coach Peahead Walker would drive to the campus in the evening, park his car by the cafeteria, and wait for the players to come out. "He'd talk to anybody who wasn't happy at Chapel Hill. That's how he got his players," Powell said. The Heels were simply overloaded with talent.

That included Holdash's position of center, which was stacked with eleven players. Holdash had an additional disadvantage in that he was from Ohio while most of the players he was competing against were from North Carolina and thus had some name recognition. Holdash understood he was simply "one of the dummies they put in there to serve as cannon fodder" for the starters. To separate himself from the pack, he decided not to be just a tackling dummy at practice. Instead, when the plays were run, he took on Ted Hazlewood with ferocity, not realizing Hazlewood was the best tackle on the team.

His strategy worked. On the third day of practice, an assistant coach told Holdash, "Consider yourself a permanent fixture. Send home, get the rest of your clothes. Tell your folks you're set here."

The long shot had made it. He went on to become an All-American center in 1950.

Matthew the tax collector was another long shot in life, an unlikely person to be a confidant of the Son of God. While we may not get all warm and fuzzy about the IRS, our government's revenue agents are nothing like Matthew and his ilk. He bought a franchise, paying the Roman Empire for the privilege of extorting, bullying, and stealing everything he could from his own people. Tax collectors of the time were "despicable, vile, unprincipled scoundrels."

And yet, Jesus said only two words to this lowlife: "Follow me." Jesus knew that this long shot would make an excellent disciple.

It's the same with us. While we may not be quite as vile as Matthew was, none of us can stand before God with our hands clean and our hearts pure. We are all impossibly long shots to enter God's Heaven. That is, until we do what Matthew did: get up and follow Jesus.

Overcoming challenges should never be considered a long shot.
-- Mother of disabled child on MightyMikeBasketball.com

Only through Jesus does our status change
from being long shots to enter God's Kingdom
to being heavy favorites.

DAY 81

DIVIDED LOYALTIES

Read Matthew 6:1-24.

"No one can serve two masters" (v. 24a).

Divided loyalties happen in the best of families; some kinfolk cheer for the Tar Heels; some holler for the Wolfpack or the Blue Devils. Few in state basketball history, though, can match the sundered loyalties Bernie Mock encountered. He is thought to be the only basketball player ever to be a team captain for both UNC and N.C. State.

The upheaval produced by World War II created Mock's unique situation. He was already a forward for the N.C. State "Red Terrors" in 1941 when the U.S. entered the war. He joined the Marine Reserve Corps in 1942 and expected to be a Red Terror in the fall. But Uncle Sam ordered him to report to UNC for V-12 training, a program established to prepare college students for military life. "I never wanted to change schools, change teams," said Mock. "But Uncle Sam said I had to go – so I went."

The eligibility rules were unique to the time, allowing athletes to play on teams based on where they were stationed. So Mock became the starting center for UNC under coach Bill Lange. "To find myself in Chapel Hill a couple of years later, playing for the rival team, that was strange," Mock said. On a train ride home from a game, Lange asked his team to elect a team captain. To Mock's surprise, his teammates voted for him. Mock went on that season to make All-Southern Conference.

Shortly after the season ended, so did Mock's playing days when he received orders to Quantico, Va., for officer's training. His legacy of divided loyalties eventually stretched across the generations. One daughter married a UNC man while his other two daughters are staunch Wolfpack fans.

Though he had an affinity for both teams, in later years Bernie Mock always had to choose where his loyalty lay when the Heels and the Wolfpack played each other. In your own life, you probably understand the stress that comes with divided loyalties. The Christian work ethic drives you to be successful. The world, however, often makes demands and presents images that conflict with your devotion to God: movies deride God; couples play musical beds in TV sitcoms; and TV dramas portray Christians as killers following God's orders.

It's Sunday morning and the office will be quiet or the golf course won't be crowded. What do you do when your heart and loyalties are pulled in two directions? Jesus knew of the struggle we face; that's why he spoke of not being able to serve "two masters," that we wind up serving one and despising the other. Put in terms of either serving God or despising God, the choice is stark and clear.

Your loyalty is to God -- always.

I felt sort of funny about it, playing against my former teammates.
-- Bernie Mock about the 1943-44 season

God does not condemn you for being successful and enjoying popular culture, but your loyalty must lie first and foremost with him.

DAY 82

LOVE STORY

Read John 15:9-17.

"My command is this: Love each other as I have loved you" (v. 12).

What in the world led Frank McGuire to leave the big-time basketball of New York City for what was then the hardcourt hinterland of Chapel Hill?

In 1952 in the city that never sleeps, McGuire was the man. A New Yorker, he had taken the St. John's Redmen to the NCAA title game. He was "one of the biggest names in college basketball. . . . McGuire knew everybody in town, and everybody returned the honor." And he up and left.

McGuire succeeded at UNC, of course, with a nine-year record of 164-58 that included five ACC titles and the legendary 1957 season when the Heels went 32-0 and defeated the Kansas Jayhawks of Wilt Chamberlain for the national title. He led UNC into the big time.

But when he arrived in 1952, he found what *Sports Illustrated* described as "bush stuff." His office was a shabby, rebuilt men's bathroom. His team crowded into private cars to travel to away games and slept on cots in the host's gym.

McGuire also had trouble recruiting players from New York City. Most of the best city players were Roman Catholic, and their coaches, parents, and sometimes even their priests warned them that to go with McGuire down to the Protestant Bible Belt was to risk losing their souls. McGuire countered by telling parents their son would be a basketball player and a missionary.

So why did he walk away from the big time? He did it for his infant son, Frankie, who was mentally handicapped and had cerebral palsy. McGuire and his wife, Pat, couldn't care for him the way they wanted to in a small apartment, and they refused to institutionalize him.

Frank McGuire gave up the city he loved for the son he loved.

To love someone is to risk betrayal and to be willing to sacrifice as Frank and Pat McGuire did in their love for their son. Since we don't take to hurt and surrender very willingly, loving other people is tough.

Yet Jesus came along and commanded – not suggested -- that we love each other. And he didn't say love only rich, good-looking folks or our children or grandchildren, who everybody knows are the cutest and smartest things in the whole world.

Jesus drew absolutely no distinctions in the depth or the breadth of his love between each one of us – grand folks that we are – and those we know who are, to put it kindly, unlovable. We are to lay down our lives for them, which doesn't mean we are to die for everybody who happens along. Rather, we are to love others in a manner that means sacrifice on our part. Even those – especially those – who aren't really lovable need love.

Once a day, do something for somebody else.

– Lou Holtz

The world desperately needs the kind of love
Jesus commands us to give: love that means giving
of ourselves and asking nothing in return.

DAY 83

PEACEMONGERS

Read Hebrews 12:14-17.

"Make every effort to live in peace with all men and to be holy" (v. 14).

After a civilized explanation of the curious new sport, the players of North Carolina and Wake Forest became uncivilized and beat each other's brains out. They kicked, crawled, pushed, pulled, fell, fumbled, and flailed at each other."

What was this "curious new sport" that was little more than a loosely organized brawl? To use the immortal words of one of UNC's most famous alums, "What it was, was football."

In the late 1880s, football was the new game in town, but it often had the appearance of one long fight. Football at UNC in those days amounted to modified rugby. A player on defense could do anything to stop the player with the ball: "tackle, trip, push, block or clip from before or behind." Such roughness "naturally led to many fights which frequently interfered with the progress of the game, and sometimes stopped it altogether until the matter at issue was settled." This was the state of the game on Oct. 18, 1888, when Wake Forest and UNC met in Raleigh in the university's first intercollegiate football game.

Pickup games on campus were also rather brutal get-togethers. Each team had fifteen on a side, but when other students showed up after play had begun, they were tossed into the fray "until each side was often composed of as many as a hundred men." Not

TAR HEELS

surprisingly, "scraps naturally became every day occurrences." When a "difficulty" inevitably arose, "the game was discontinued, a circle was made in the center of the field, the contending parties placed therein and made to settle their dispute in a free-for-all and fist-to-fist scrap." As soon as one player won the fight, "the game was again resumed as though nothing out of the ordinary had occurred."

Such was football at Chapel Hill in its early days, a game one writer succinctly described as a "barbarous affair."

Perhaps you've never been in a brawl or a public brouhaha to match that of those pioneer Tar Heel football players, but maybe you retaliated when you got one elbow too many in a pickup basketball game. Or maybe you and your spouse or your teenager get into it occasionally, shouting and saying cruel things. Or road rage may be a part of your life.

While we do seem to live in a more belligerent, confrontational society than ever before, fighting is still not the solution to a problem. Rather, it only escalates the whole confrontation, leaving wounded pride, intransigence, and simmering hatred in its wake. Actively seeking and making peace is the way to a solution that lasts and heals broken relationships and aching hearts.

Peacemaking is not as easy as fighting, but it is much more courageous and a lot less painful. It is also the Jesus thing to do.

It was a rough game.
-- *Early UNC football player Charles Baskerville*

**Making peace instead of fighting takes courage
and strength; it's also what Jesus would do.**

DAY 84

MYSTERIOUS WAYS

Read Romans 11:25-36.

"O the depth of the riches and wisdom and knowledge of God! How unsearchable are his judgments and how inscrutable his ways!" (v. 33 NRSV)

On the Monday after Carolina's regional final win over Wisconsin in 2005, the players showed up for what they thought would be practice as usual. Instead, they found a mystery.

Sean May's 29 points and 12 rebounds led the Heels past the Badgers 88-82 and into the Final Four in St. Louis. Coach Roy Williams knew his team could play better, though, and would need to, especially on the defensive end. Thus, the mystery.

What had the players looking quizzically at each other that Monday was a 35-minute segment of the practice labeled simply "The Pit." The players went through their shooting drills and some fast-break drills when Williams announced, "Let's go to The Pit." He led his team into the practice gym where the players spotted something rather ominous: The rims had been removed from the backboards, which only deepened the mystery.

It was solved when the coaches put them through 35 minutes of defensive drills. No shooting, no dribbling, just defense. May said he was frustrated by the missing rims, but understood what was happening: "Coach was trying to instill that defensive mentality again because that's what was going to make us successful."

When the intense drills ended, Williams promised his players they would be back the next day. "We're going to be better defensively in St. Louis," he declared.

After the time in The Pit, Williams was convinced there would be no mystery about how the team would play defensively. He said the two games in St. Louis "were maybe our two best defensive games of the year." They were certainly good enough to win a national championship.

We often love a good mystery because we relish the challenge of uncovering what somebody else wants to hide. We are intrigued by a perplexing whodunit, a rousing round of Clue, or *Matlock* reruns.

Unlike The Pit and what it held for the Heels, some mysteries are simply beyond our knowing. Much about life that is in actuality the mysterious ways of God remains hidden from our understanding and comprehension because we can't see the divine machinations. We can see only the results, appreciate that God was behind it all, and give him thanks and praise.

God has revealed much about himself, especially through Jesus, but still much remains unknowable. Why does he tolerate the existence of evil? What does he really look like? Why is he so fond of bugs? We know for certain, though, that God is love, and so we proceed with life, assured that one day all mysteries will be revealed.

I think The Pit really helped us.

– Sean May

**God chooses to keep much about himself
shrouded in mystery, but one day
we will see and we will understand.**

MEMORY LOSS

Read 1 Corinthians 11:17-29.

"[D]o this in remembrance of me" (v. 24).

Scott Stankavage remembered very well. How could he forget the "most controversial, debilitating, momentum-wrecking game" of the last twenty-five-plus years.

Stankavage was the quarterback on Oct. 29, 1983, when the Heels played Maryland up there. UNC was 7-0 and ranked third in the nation with a team that included future NFL stars Ethan Horton and Harris Barton.

With 22 seconds left, the Heels scored to trail 28-26 and lined up for the two-point conversion to tie. Facing them was a mob of "frothing students" at the back of the end zone. Stankavage's pass for running back Tyrone Anthony was incomplete. "As the pass went off Anthony's fingertips," longtime Carolina broadcaster Woody Durham remembered, "he just disappeared into a sea of students." The Maryland students poured onto the field and tore down both goalposts before officials could clear them so the teams could finish the game. Two ambulances and a helicopter evacuated several injured fans.

The Heels appeared to recover an onsides kick, which brought up an interesting dilemma: What would the officials have done with a field-goal attempt? But the officials talked it over at length and awarded the ball to Maryland, which ran out the clock.

School officials didn't forget; they sniped at each other for more than a week. UNC Coach Dick Crum later said that Maryland administrators should use "barbed wire and land mines" "to ensure that students didn't pull a similar stunt in the future."

Stankavage and Durham and other UNC fans remember well that game because as Durham said, "The bottom fell out after that," slamming Carolina into a "puzzling" skid. The team lost four of its last five games and Crum was soon gone; not until 1996 would the Heels appear again in the Top 10.

Memory makes us who we are. Whether our memories are dreams or nightmares, they shape us and to a large extent determine our actions and reactions. Alzheimer's is so terrifying because it steals our memory from us and in the process we lose ourselves. We disappear.

The greatest tragedy of our lives is that God remembers. In response to that memory, he condemns us for our sin. On the other hand, the greatest joy of our lives is that God remembers. In response to that memory, he came as Jesus to wash even the memory of our sins away.

Through memory, we encounter revival. At the Last Supper, Jesus instructed his disciples and us to remember. In sharing this unique meal with fellow believers and remembering Jesus and his actions, we meet Christ again not just as a memory but as an actual living presence. To remember is to keep our faith alive.

I think people forget how good we were then. I mean, we were No. 3 in the country.

-- Scott Stankavage

We remember Jesus, and God will not remember our sins.

THE RIGHT PERSON

Read Matthew 26:47-50; 27:1-10.

*"The betrayer had arranged a signal with them: 'The one I
kiss is the man; arrest him.' Going at once to Jesus, Judas
said, 'Greetings, Rabbi!' and kissed him" (vv. 48-49).*

They hanged him in effigy and called for his firing. Who was
this man many people felt wasn't the right man for the job? Dean
Smith.

An assistant to Frank McGuire for three seasons, Smith was a
virtual unknown when he took over the UNC men's basketball
program in August 1961. Chancellor William Aycock conceded
he hired Smith in part because of his lack of stature. Aycock and
Smith both knew, too, that other than the chancellor, the new
coach's support was "virtually nonexistent."

By Smith's fourth season, except among his players, the
"virtually" could probably have been omitted when speaking of
the coach's support. The Heels went 8-9, 15-6, and 12-12 those
first three seasons. Years later, Duke All-American Art Heyman
recalled that at the time Smith "was the biggest joke around."
Even Smith wrestled with getting out.

Charlie Shaffer, who played on Smith's first three teams, was
"appalled at the things people called Smith right to his face. I
thought, 'How can he stand this?'" Larry Brown, the best player
on Smith's first team, said, "I don't know how many men could
have gone through those first few years." After a 107-85 drubbing

TAR HEELS

by Wake Forest dropped Smith's fourth team to 6-6, the team bus arrived at Woollen Gym to find an effigy of Smith hanging over the front door. The main question now had become not whether Smith would leave but who would replace him.

Then a few days later, in Durham, the Heels beat Duke 65-62. This time when the team returned, a crowd cheered for Smith to speak.

Folks had finally begun to realize that Dean Smith was the right man for the job after all.

What do you want to be when you grow up? Somehow you are supposed to know the answer to that question when you're a teenager, the time in life when common sense and logic are at their lowest ebb. Long after those halcyon teen years are left behind, you may make frequent career changes. You chase the job that gives you not just financial rewards but also some personal satisfaction and sense of accomplishment. You desire a profession that uses your abilities, that you enjoy doing, and that gives you a sense of contributing to something bigger than yourself.

God, too, wants you in the right job, one that he has designed specifically for you. After all, even Judas was the right man for what God needed done. To do his work, God gave you abilities, talents, and passions. Do what you do best and what you love -- just do it for God.

Coach Smith was a case of the right man at the right time.
-- Former UNC Chancellor William Aycock

God has a job for you, one for which he gave you particular talents, abilities, and passions.

DAY 87

DANCING MACHINE

Read 2 Samuel 6:12-22.

"David danced before the Lord with all his might, while he and the entire house of Israel brought up the ark of the Lord with shouts and the sound of trumpets" (vv. 14-15).

Before the national title game, Coach Anson Dorrance had to run his 2008 women's soccer team out of the locker room. Were they intimidated? Slacking off? Nah; they were just dancing.

Dorrance confessed he had to shoo his players out before the title game with Notre Dame on Dec. 6 "because they were all dancing" and he "was afraid we weren't going to warm up for the match." The legendary coach was delighted with the whole business. "They have been so much fun," he said about his team. "This is one of the most incredible falls I've ever had in my life."

The 2008 team members were so loose before the title game because they entered it in an unusual position for the greatest dynasty in the history of college sports (See devotion No. 12); they weren't supposed to be there. "Our route to a championship was to beat two undefeated teams," Dorrance said. "We were the spoiler." And so as strange as it may sound, by doing all that dancing the Heels "were celebrating the fact that we were finally the underdogs. What a joyful place to compete from."

It didn't make any difference in the outcome. UNC beat the first undefeated team, UCLA, 1-0, and then came from behind in the finals to beat the 26-0 Irish for the championship. It looked as though Notre Dame might put an embarrassment on the team with no expectations when they scored only 16 seconds into the game. But, said goalkeeper Ashlyn Harris, "Right after they scored, we just went at them." Casey Nogueira, the national player of the year, scored a pair of last-half goals for a 2-1 win and another national championship.

Which set off another round of dancing.

One of the more enduring stereotypes of the Christian is of a dour, sour-faced person always on the prowl to sniff out fun and frivolity and shut it down. "Somewhere, sometime, somebody's having fun – and it's got to stop!" Many understand this to be the mandate that governs the Christian life.

But nothing could be further from reality. Long ago King David, he who numbered Jesus Christ among his house and lineage, set the standard for those who love and worship the Lord when he danced in the presence of God with unrestrained joy. Many centuries and one savior later, David's example today reminds us that a life spent in an awareness of God's presence is all about celebrating, rejoicing, and enjoying God's countless gifts, including salvation in Jesus Christ.

Yes, dancing can be vulgar and coarse, but as with David, God looks into our hearts to see what is there. Our very life should be one long song and dance for Jesus.

Dancers are the athletes of God.

-- Albert Einstein

**While dancing and music can be
vulgar and obscene, they can also be
inspiring expressions of abiding love for God.**

DAY 88

CALLING IT QUITS

Read Numbers 13:25-14:4.

"The men who had gone up with him said, 'We can't attack those people; they are stronger than we are'" (v. 13:31).

Chris Keldorf told his dad he was quitting football. That was, of course, before he led the Heels to a 21-3 record and put his name all over the school record book.

Keldorf was the starter for Mack Brown's 10-2 Gator-Bowl champions of 1996 and was first-team All-ACC. He shared playing time with junior Oscar Davenport in 1997, starting seven of the twelve games.

Against TCU his senior season, Keldorf set a school record by throwing for 415 yards passing. He threw for 290 yards and three touchdowns and was the MVP in a 42-3 demolishing of Virginia Tech in the Gator Bowl. The Heels finished 11-1 and ranked fourth in the nation. In his two seasons at Chapel Hill, Keldorf set school records for career touchdown passes, career completions per game, and completions per game in a season.

Only Utah State offered Keldorf a scholarship out of high school, and he took it. Former Seattle Seahawks quarterback Jim Zorn was on the staff and told Keldorf he would never be a quarterback and should move to tight end. Instead, Keldorf transferred to a junior college only to find future BYU star Steve Sarkisian there.

That's when Keldorf decided to pack it in. His dad talked him out of it, though, telling him, "You don't want to be 40 years old and wish you had given it a shot." Keldorf moved again, to another junior college, where eventually Brown and assistant coach Cleve Bryant, desperate for a quarterback after the corps was depleted by graduation and injuries, found him and brought him to Carolina.

After that, he quit only because he had used up his eligibility while becoming one of the most successful quarterbacks in Tar Heel history.

Remember that time you quit a high-school sports team? Bailed out of a relationship? Walked away from that job with the goals unachieved? Sometimes quitting is the most sensible way to minimize your losses, so you may well at times in your life give up on something or someone.

In your relationship with God, however, you should remember the people of Israel, who quit when the Promised Land was theirs for the taking. They forgot one fact of life you never should: God never gives up on you.

That means you should never, ever give up on God. No matter how tired or discouraged you get, no matter that it seems your prayers aren't getting through to God, no matter what – quitting on God is not an option. He is preparing a blessing for you, and in his time, he will bring it to fruition -- if you don't quit on him.

The first time you quit, it's hard. The second time, it gets easier. The third time, you don't even have to think about it.

-- *Bear Bryant*

Whatever else you give up on in your life, don't give up on God; he will never ever give up on you.

DAY 89

PAIN RELIEF

Read 2 Corinthians 1:3-7.

"Just as the sufferings of Christ flow over into our lives, so also through Christ our comfort overflows" (v. 5).

Phil Ford couldn't dunk and wasn't particularly fast, but he could sure play with pain.

He was a three-time All-America and the national player of the year as a senior in 1978. He left school as Carolina's all-time leading scorer with 2,290 points; his record was eventually broken by Tyler Hansbrough. His number – 12 – is retired.

Ford was the master of Dean Smith's Four Corners offense; "when the 6-2 point guard held four fingers up high with his left hand while dribbling with his right, the game was over."

He never dunked in a game. "I sort of half-dunked once in a pep rally," he said. "Since that's the only time I got up that high, I'm counting it." He also admitted he wasn't particularly fast, at least in a 100-yard dash. "But in a five-yard dash, you'd have a hard time beating me."

He was talented and he was tough. His reaction during an ACC Tournament game against Clemson his sophomore season of 1976 is among the legends of UNC basketball. Telling the story matter-of-factly, Ford said, "Stan Rome elbowed me in the mouth and knocked one of my teeth out. I kept my dribble alive, handed the tooth to the trainer, and kept on playing."

Dean Smith recounted the incident repeatedly over the years as an example of grace under pressure. In the late 1980s, when Ford as an assistant coach was often in the locker room, All-American J.R. Reid would frequently joke about how the story had grown with the retelling. He would rhetorically ask Smith to "tell us about the time that Coach Ford jumped on a bomb while he was on the court, got his arm blown off, kept his dribble alive, and kept on playing."

That, of course, was a humorous exaggeration. The true story, though, illustrates clearly that Phil Ford could play with pain.

Since you live on Earth and not in Heaven, you are forced to play with pain. Whether it's a car wreck that left you shattered, the end of a relationship that left you battered, or a loved one's death that left you tattered -- pain finds you and challenges you to keep going.

While God's word teaches that you will reap what you sow, life also teaches that pain and hardship are not necessarily the result of personal failure. Pain in fact can be one of the tools God uses to mold your character and change your life.

What are you to do when you are hit full-speed by the awful pain that seems to choke the very will to live out of you? Where is your consolation, your comfort, and your help?

In almighty God, whose love will never fail. When life knocks you to your knees, you're closer to God than ever before.

It hurts up to a point and then it doesn't get any worse.
-- Ultramarathon runner Ann Trason

When life hits you with pain, you can always turn to God for comfort, consolation, and hope.

DAY 90

CELEBRATION TIME

Read Exodus 14:26-31; 15:19-21.

"Miriam the prophetess, Aaron's sister, took a tambourine in her hand, and all the women followed her, with tambourines and dancing" (v. 15:20).

On Sunday, March 24, 1957, a form of mass hysteria appeared to seize the citizens of North Carolina. . . . All across the state, people suddenly rushed out of their houses and began to dance in the streets. [They yelled and] built bonfires in the public squares. School and firehouse bells rang out, and hastily assembled street bands blared rousing southern marches."

Such was the celebration unleashed by UNC's win over Kansas in the NCAA Tournament championship game.

In Chapel Hill, 2,000 people poured into the streets "hanging out of trees and on the side of lampposts." A man jumped up and down on top of a car, shouting and waving his arms. When the crowd saw him, they gave a raucous cheer. The joyous person was the university's chancellor, who took the unprecedented step of allowing coeds to stay out until 2:00 a.m. to celebrate the win.

As the team flight neared Raleigh the following night, the "biggest traffic jam in North Carolina history was building." A line of cars stretched eighteen miles from the airport to Chapel Hill, and the crowd swelled to an estimated 10,000 people.

The players had no idea what was going on. "I don't think any of us envisioned what we saw when we looked out the window," recalled starting guard Tommy Kearns. "It was extraordinary." One participant called the celebration "crazy but not riotous. It was just a mass of people who were all deliriously happy."

After "signing endless autographs, shaking countless hands, and walking through a hail of signs and confetti," the champions eventually made it to Chapel Hill where another crowd greeted them, and the celebration continued.

You know what it takes to throw a good party. You start with your closest friends, add some salsa and chips, fire up the grill and throw on some burgers and dogs, and then top it all off with the UNC game on TV.

You probably also know that any old excuse will do to get people together for a celebration. All you really need is a sense that life is pretty good right now.

That's the thing about having Jesus as part of your life: He turns every day into a celebration of the good life. No matter what tragedies or setbacks life may have in store, the heart given to Jesus will find the joy in living. That's because such a life is spent with quiet confidence in God's promise of salvation through Jesus, a confidence that inevitably bubbles up into a joy the troubles of the world cannot touch.

When a life is celebrated with Jesus, the party never stops.

This is worse than V-J Day.
— A Chapel Hill policeman surveying the celebration
after the championship win

With Jesus, life is one big party because it becomes a celebration of victory and joy.

NOTES
(by Devotion Day Number)

1   Five boys from Charlotte "just got together one day and started it.": Ken Rappaport, *Tar Heel: North Carolina Basketball* (Huntsville, AL: The Strode Publishers, 1976), p. 16.

1   Basketball originally arrived on campus . . . with pursuing, panting faculty members." Rappaport, *Tar Heel: North Carolina Basketball*, p. 14.

1   For several years, the game lacked any formal structure at UNC.: Rappaport, *Tar Heel: North Carolina Basketball*, p. 15.

1   In 1910, five Charlotte students . . . schedule some games with other colleges.: Rappaport, *Tar Heel: North Carolina Basketball*, p. 16.

1   the athletic association was so . . . to hire a separate coach.: Rappaport, *Tar Heel: North Carolina Basketball*, p. 13.

1   despite having to practice outdoors . . . was configured for track.: Rappaport, *Tar Heel: North Carolina Basketball*, p. 16.

1   The sport wasn't exactly received with "a raging fever.": Rappaport, *Tar Heel: North Carolina Basketball*, p. 14.

1   "There wasn't much enthusiasm for basketball then,": Rappaport, *Tar Heel: North Carolina Basketball*, p. 17.

1   "If we had 35 or 40 . . . it was pretty good.": Rappaport, *Tar Heel: North Carolina Basketball*, p. 14.

2   the post office would deliver . . . "Choo Choo, NC.": Ken Rappaport, *Tar Heel: North Carolina Football* (Huntsville, AL: The Strode Publishers, 1976), p. 23.

2   "He was a bonafide superstar . . . a legend in his own time.": "Charlie 'Choo-Choo' Justice," *Carolina Football: 2008 Media Guide*, p. 132, http://tarheelblue.cstv.com/sports/m-footbl/spec-rel/072708aaa.html, July 10, 2009.

2   Hundreds of babies were named for him.: Rappaport, *Tar Heel: North Carolina Football*, p. 26.

2   The legendary Benny Goodman . . . "All the Way Choo Choo": "Charlie 'Choo-Choo' Justice."

2   that sold 50,000 copies. . . . the other 58 named Justice.: Rappaport, *Tar Heel: North Carolina Football*, p. 26.

2   "women, young and old, . . . football player to celebrity.": Rappaport, *Tar Heel: North Carolina Football*, p. 27.

2   Fame is strange. . . . is never your own.: Rappaport, *Tar Heel: North Carolina Football*, p. 83.

3   The Tar Heels were seeded . . . had ever won the title.: "Carolina History," *2009 UNC Men's Lacrosse Media Guide*, p. 35, http://grfx.cstv.com/photos/schools/unc/sports/m-lacros/auto_pdf/unc09-mlaxmg.pdf, July 16, 2009.

4   Coach Roy Williams said it would haunt him forever.: Tim Layden, "Promise Fulfilled," *Sports Illustrated*, April 15, 2009, http://vault.sportsillustrated.cnn.com/vault/article/magazine/MAG1154814/index.htm, June 30, 2009.

4   forward Tyler Hansbrough wouldn't watch . . . worst game of his life.: Layden, "Promise Fulfilled."

4   "a ruthless assault that transformed . . . in here with anything left.": Layden, "Promise Fulfilled."

4   Remember what happened last year.: Layden, "Promise Fulfilled."

5   On a recruiting visit, Smith . . . apart from the rest." Scott Fowler, *Where Have You Gone?* (Champaign, IL: Sports Publishing L.L.C., 2005), p. 99.

5   "I have a great take . . . All that started at Carolina.": Fowler, p. 100.

6   But after two time outs, . . . Smith on the right wing.: Stephanie Lawrence Yelton, "1994 NCAA Championship Game: UNC 60, Louisiana Tech 59," *2008-09 UNC*

Women's Basketball Media Guide, p. 100, http://tarheelblue.cstv.com/sports/w-baskbl/spec-rel/111308aae.html, July 13, 2009.

6   "I didn't look at it . . . I knew it had gone in.": Yelton, p. 100.

6   Smith had to wait and watch the replay: Yelton, p. 100.

6   setting an NCAA championship game record.: "Retired and Honored Jerseys at UNC: Charlotte Smith #23," *2008-09 UNC Women's Basketball Media Guide*, p. 104, http://tarheelblue.cstv.com/sports/w-baskbl/spec-rel/111308aae.html, July 13, 2009.

7   His dreams were "wrapped up in basketball.": Tim Crothers, "Game of Choice," *Sports Illustrated*, Aug. 13, 2001, http://vault.sportsillustated.cnn.com/vault/article/magazine/MAG1023179/index.htm, June 30, 2009.

7   he had his own mail slot . . . walk on to the basketball team.: Crothers.

7   "Julius was a godsend, the missing piece for us,": Crothers.

7   to his surprise Peppers found himself looking forward to football.: Crothers.

8   Worthy was the team's best player.: Jimmy Black with Scott Fowler, *Jimmy Black's Tales from the Tar Heels* (Champaign, IL: Sports Publishing L.L.C., 2006), p. 16.

8   Worthy wasn't looking for . . . a dent in the floor.": Black with Fowler, p. 91.

8   "took off from [the] foul . . . move over for Dr. James.": Black with Fowler, p. 90.

8   the Heels trailed 49-45 . . . dunk on Sleepy Floyd's head.": Black with Fowler, p. 101.

9   Head coach Frank McGuire "prepared . . . two-hour blackboard sessions.": Rappaport, *Tar Heel: North Carolina Basketball*, p. 107.

10   were played on a field just east . . . those stands burned in 1909.: "Before Kenan Stadium and Before Emerson Field," http://www.ramfanatic.com/Football/before_kenan_stadium_and_before_.htm, July 17, 2009.

10   In 1914, Isaac Edward Emerson, . . . athletic field for baseball and football.: "Bromo-Seltzer," *Sour Stomachs and Galloping Headaches*, http://www.lib.unc.edu/ncc/ssgh/strong.html, July 17, 2009.

10   On the site of what is . . . and the Student Union,: David E. Brown, "Southern Beauty," *UNC General Alumni Association*, http://alumni.unc.edu/article.aspx?SID=572, July 17, 2009.

10   "Down in one corner . . . you were punting uphill.": Rappaport, *Tar Heel: North Carolina Football*, p. 118.

10   even with the addition of some wooden bleachers,: Rappaport, *Tar Heel: North Carolina Football*, p. 118.

10   by 1921, the university . . . thousands of paying customers.: Rappaport, *Tar Heel: North Carolina Football*, p. 119.

10   Expansion would ruin the site for baseball,: "UNC Kenan Stadium – 'America's Most Beautiful Stadium,'" http://www.sports-venue.info/NCAAF/Kenan_Stadium.html, July 17, 2009.

10   the construction to be funded from alumni donations.: "UNC Kenan Stadium."

10   Fundraising didn't go too well: Brown.

10   I was not prepared to find the stadium as beautiful as it is.: Brown.

11   "went into a maniacal, . . . on Johnson's scoring record.: Steve Elling, "A Fullback's Moment of Glory," *The News & Observer*, Oct. 10, 1996, http://docs.newsbank.com/s/InfoWeb/aggdocs/NewsBank/0EB03599E8533E36, Aug. 11, 2009.

12   No less an expert than . . . calling the success "astounding.": Chris Ballard, "The Program," *Sports Illustrated on Campus*, Nov. 6, 2003, http:/vault.sportsillustrated.cnn.com/vault/article/web/COM1001589/index.htm, July 14, 2009.

12   "have hoarded national and conference . . . respect befitting a dynasty.": "Head Coach Anson Dorrance," *2008 UNC Women's Soccer Media Guide*, p. 34, http://tarheelblue.cstv.com/auto_pdf/p_hotos/s_chools/unc/sports/w-soccer/auto_pdf/08-w-soccer-mg, July 14, 2009.

12   UNC is not a basketball school but a women's soccer school.: Ballard.

13   That evening back in . . . all over Franklin Street.: Fowler, p. 124.

13   As a child, his home situation . . . in an alcohol-fueled rage: Fowler, p. 123.

13   she didn't even recall. She died in 2004.: Fowler, p. 124.

13   "He had money, plenty of free time, . . . turned to the Bible: Fowler, p. 123.

13   "The most gratifying thing . . . speak about God's love,": Fowler, p. 123.

13   "was meant to be a blessing to someone else.": Fowler, p. 125.

14   who earlier in the game had . . . a water-bucket bath on the sideline.: A.J. Carr, "Heels win by a Little," *The News & Observer*, Nov. 25, 2007, http://www.newsobserver.com/front/story/791984.html, July 29, 2009.

14   Little suggested a play. . . . laid down their blocks,: Carr.

15   Starter Charlie Shaffer recalled . . . guys go four-on-four.": Frank Deford, "Long Ago, He Won the Big One," *Sports Illustrated*, Nov. 19, 1982, http://vault.sportsillustrated.cnn.com/vault/article/magazine/MAG1126178/index.htm, June 30, 2009.

16   "Could you imagine how many . . . get him to relax,": Alexander Wolff, "Dean Emeritus," *Sports Illustrated*, Oct. 20, 1997, http://sportsillustrated.cnn.com/vault/article/magazine/MAG1011148/index.htm, Aug. 12, 2009.

16   By late August, Guthridge said, . . . and he wasn't quite ready.": Wolff, "Dean Emeritus."

16   The late date meant . . . cupboard was well stocked.: Wolff, "Dean Emeritus."

16   This'll be really big . . . retires tomorrow, that is.: Wolff, "Dean Emeritus."

17   "Chad was huge," . . . to the backs ahead of him.: Phil Taylor, "Shocking Blue," *Sports Illustrated*, Nov. 8, 2004, http://vault.sportsillustrated.cnn.com/vault/article/magazine/MAG1113619/index.htm, June 30, 2009.

17   "Our offensive line is the . . . through the celebrating Carolina mob.: Taylor.

18   "What if we did it?" . . . That would be a Carolina basketball story.": Adam Lucas, Steve Kirschner, and Matt Bowers, *Led by Their Dreams* (Guilford, CN: The Lyons Press, 2005), p. 121.

18   "How else could it have ended?" . . . We're champions.": Lucas, Kirschner, and Bowers, p. 112.

18   Winning the championship was a dream come true.: Lucas, Kirschner, and Bowers, p. 165.

19   He failed to make his . . . a tryout with North Carolina State,: Fowler, p. 3.

19   "For me, it was hot," . . . without breathing heavily.": Fowler, p. 4.

19   That same talent scout, . . . without ever seeing him play.: Fowler, p. 4.

20   "a redneck, an Englishman, a Yankee and Noz": Mark Bechtel, "Great Briton," *Sports Illustrated*, Dec. 24, 2001, http://vault.sportsillustrated.cnn.com/vault/article/magazine/MAG1024608/index.htm, June 30, 2009.

20   Senior goalkeeper Mike Ueltchey offered . . . and became best friends,": Bechtel.

20   Intercollegiate sports remain almost . . . "an eager reply.": Bechtel.

21   he could put both elbows on the rim while dunking the ball.: Fowler, p. 46.

21   His final choices came down to Duke and UNC.: Fowler, p. 48.

21   "When Miller came, that . . . the whole thing around,: Fowler, p. 49.

21   until 1974 when he left . . . the one course he needed.: Fowler, p. 50.

22   Gore started out playing second . . . don't care where I play.'": Rachel Ullrich, "UNC's Gore a True Role Player," *The News & Observer*, May 19, 2009, http://www.newsobserver.com/sports/college/unc/story/1533227.html, July 27, 2009.

23   "a championship factory" . . . kicked around in recent years.": Rappaport, *Tar Heel: North Carolina Football*, p. 171.

23   "a stalking sideline presence . . . We won 21-7.": Rappaport, *Tar Heel: North Carolina Football*, p. 162.

23   Tatum believed his team would be a powerhouse.: Rappaport, *Tar Heel: North Carolina Football*, p. 172.

23   No one knows when he . . . in the blink of an eye.": Jim & Julie S. Bettinger, *The Book of Bowden* (Nashville: TowleHouse Publishing, 2001), p. 21.

24   A football injury left . . . he never fully recovered.: Rappaport, *Tar Heel: North*

24   *Carolina Basketball*, pp. 54, 56.

24   "I designed a Braille system . . . and shot from there.": Rappaport, *Tar Heel: North Carolina Basketball*, p. 56.

24   Teammate Lew Hayworth said Glamack . . . the reason he made all-America.: Rappaport, *Tar Heel: North Carolina Basketball*, p. 56.

24   Glamack tried contact lenses, . . . eyes started to burn.": Rappaport, *Tar Heel: North Carolina Basketball*, p. 59.

24   It's amazing. Some of the . . . true to be a Christian man.: Bettinger, p. 121.

25   FSU guard Sam Cassell had derided . . . after a Seminole win.: Warren Hynes, "A Comeback Made for Record Books," *The Year in Review: 1993 National Champions* (Chapel Hill: The Daily Tar Heel, 1993), p. 34.

25   "woofing in the locker . . . couldn't guard him.: Fowler, p. 153.

25   "The 3-pointers began to fall, . . . FSU led by a single point,": Hynes, "A Comeback," p. 34.

25   He stole a pass and . . . on the school's all-time list.: Hynes, "A Comeback" p. 34.

25   "They're not a wine-and-cheese crowd anymore.": Hynes, "A Comeback," p. 34.

26   In the second game of that . . . dogmatic students" joined him: Rappaport, *Tar Heel: North Carolina Football*, p. 99.

26   convinced the trustees to reverse . . . Prof. Williams as its chairman.: Rappaport, *Tar Heel: North Carolina Football*, p. 100.

26   As it stands now, . . . to advance athletics.: Rappaport, *Tar Heel: North Carolina Football*, p. 99.

27   They didn't have any great goals.": Rappaport, *Tar Heel: North Carolina Basketball*, p. 159.

27   having to practice at night . . . classes and intramural teams.: Rappaport, *Tar Heel: North Carolina Basketball*, p. 133.

27   "magnificent basketball palace" . . . had no such plan.: Rappaport, *Tar Heel: North Carolina Basketball*, pp. 131, 133.

27   "This has been the worst year of my life.": Rappaport, *Tar Heel: North Carolina Basketball*, p. 147.

27   which "proved to be a knockout punch" for McGuire.: Rappaport, *Tar Heel: North Carolina Basketball*, p. 147.

27   an embarrassed administration responded . . . McGuire resigned.: Rappaport, *Tar Heel: North Carolina Basketball*, p. 148.

27   with only one mandate: . . . have a basketball program, period.": Rappaport, *Tar Heel: North Carolina Basketball*, p. 159.

27   I always wanted to be a coach.: Rappaport, *Tar Heel: North Carolina Basketball*, p. 161.

28   "He's done as much positive . . . a pair of praying hands.": Steve Elling, "Departing Deas Leaves His Mark," *The News & Observer*, Aug. 18, 1998, http://us.mg2.mail.yahoo.com/dc/launch?.gx+1&.rand=31c9flivb1geh, Aug. 12, 2009.

28   "He meant a lot of things to a lot of people,": Elling, "Departing Deas."

28   "His purpose here, it . . . a higher plane, spiritual,": Elling, "Departing Deas."

29   the "cable network ESPN2 . . . the hook to sell subscriptions.: Art Chansky, *Blue Blood* (New York: Thomas Dunne Books, 2006), p. 242.

29   C.D. Chesley played freshman football . . . twenty stations that first season.: Chansky, p. 243.

29   Life is an adventure. . . . going to happen next.: Bettinger, p. 74.

30   "George was so good, . . . picked [him at tackle,": Rappaport, *Tar Heel: North Carolina Football*, p. 136.

30   While Shaffer called the signals . . . plays I've ever seen,": Rappaport, *Tar Heel: North Carolina Football*, p. 137.

30   Prior to the 1934 Cavalier . . his spiffy new suit.: Rappaport, *Tar Heel: North Carolina Football*, p. 135.

31   "I was hanging out on . . . Pepper got it,": Fowler, p. 120.

31	Pepper, 45, was still playing . . . very uneasy, awkward feeling.": Fowler, p. 116.
31	"Most people in his situation would have died,": Fowler, p. 119.
31	"I'm so thankful the good Lord looked after me,": Fowler, p. 119.
32	watching proudly was Ty's father, . . . quality father-son time,": Gene Menez, "Danger: Highly Explosive," *Sports Illustrated*, April 15, 2009, http://vault.sportsil-lustrated.cnn.com/vault/article/magazine/MAG1154819/index.htm, June 30, 2009.
33	The origins of his startling . . . fingers off his right hand.: Rappaport, *Tar Heel: North Carolina Basketball*, p. 13.
33	"ran like a choo-choo train on a snaking, uneven track.": Rappaport, *Tar Heel: North Carolina Football*, p. 15.
33	The "B.V.D Boys" of 1967-68 earned . . . they won the tournament.: Rappaport, *Tar Heel: North Carolina Football*, p. 188.
33	The squad actually had seventeen backs,: Rappaport, *Tar Heel: North Carolina Football*, p. 120.
33	One legend derives from . . . they have tar on their heels.": "Why Tar Heels?" *Carolina Football: 2009 Football Media Guide*, p. 208, http://tarheelblue.cstv.com/sports/m-footbl-spec-rel/072809aab.html, Aug. 7, 2009.
34	"developed into maybe the best . . . about moving on out,": Caulton Tudor, "Fisher Hopes to Deliver On-Field Message, Too," *The News & Observer*, Aug. 22, 1998, http://us.mg2mail.yahoo.com/dc/launch?.gx=1&.rand=3qlsitdj8n7pl, Aug. 7, 2009.
34	"I was partying all the time," . . . Tar Heels' Bible study leader.: Tudor, "Fisher Hopes."
34	"The Lord took care of things for me,": Tudor, "Fisher Hopes."
35	Jamison came to North Carolina . . . woman he called Mama.: Alexander Wolff, "No Question," *Sports Illustrated*, Feb. 16, 1998, http://sportsillustrated.cnn.com/vault/article/magaine/MAG1011982/2/index.htm, Aug. 12, 2009.
36	As the opening game of what . . . a freshman named Jordan.: Black with Fowler, p. 47.
36	"the most famous play in Tar . . . most famous in college athletics.": "1982 NCAA Champions," *2008-09 Carolina Basketball Media Guide*, p. 115, http://tarheelblue.cstv.com/auto/pdf/p_hotos/s_chools/unc/sports/m-baskbl/auto_pdf, July 16, 2009.
36	"launched Michael Jordan as the greatest player in the sport's history.": "1982 NCAA Champions."
36	The competition was between . . . at least four inches taller." Black with Fowler, p. 47.
36	Jordan joined Phil Ford, . . . had ever started in season openers.: Black with Fowler, p. 48.
36	"You could already see . . . with [Jordan] starting.": Black with Fowler, p. 49.
36	Michael really won the job with his defense.: Black with Fowler, p. 48.
37	"Ivy" – as the homefolks call her . . . some scenes from *The Patriot*.: Martha Quil-lin, "Town Loves Its Girl Latta," *The News & Observer*, April 1, 2006, http://www.newsobserver.com/front/story/424211.html, July 30, 2009.
38	Coach Bill Dooley called McCauley "the greatest football player I've ever seen.": Rappaport, *Tar Heel: North Carolina Football*, p. 210.
38	recurring nightmares kept him awake . . . would not let him break away.: Rappaport, *Tar Heel: North Carolina Football*, p. 210.
38	thirteen more carries than . . . carried him across the field.: Rappaport, *Tar Heel: North Carolina Football*, p. 210.
39	In November 1992, Coach Dean Smith . . . it'll be in New Orleans,": Warren Hynes, "A Season Built on Believing," *The Year in Review: 1993 National Champions*, Chapel Hill: *The Daily Tar Heel*, 1993, p. 24.
39	They saw the future, pure and simple. It was already written down.: Hynes, "A Season Built on Believing," p. 24.
40	The team was later recognized as the national champion.: Rappaport, *Tar Heel: North Carolina Basketball*, p. 29.

40	The 1924 team acquired its unique . . . ghost-like moves of the players.: Rappaport, *Tar Heel: North Carolina Basketball*, p. 40.
40	some writers accused them of showboating. . . . made the opponents look awkward.: Rappaport, *Tar Heel: North Carolina Basketball*, p. 29.
40	in an age when . . . considered a good game.: Rappaport, *Tar Heel: North Carolina Basketball*, p. 32.
40	"established Carolina as the team . . . pretty consistently ever since.": Rappaport, *Tar Heel: North Carolina Basketball*, p. 40.
41	players let their hair . . . they didn't wear helmets.: Clyde Bolton, *War Eagle* (Huntsville, AL: The Strode Publishers, 1973), p. 45.
41	The ball was shaped . . . your hand and pass.: Clyde Bolton, *The Crimson Tide* (Huntsville, AL: The Strode Publishers, 1972), p. 46.
41	Games were called on account of darkness.: Bolton, *War Eagle*, p. 48.
41	A nose guard was about . . . he provided them himself.: Bolton, *The Crimson Tide*, p. 46.
41	Teams sometimes scrambled to find . . . rather than a level one.: Bolton, *War Eagle*, p. 50.
41	A player hid . . . No scoreboard.: Bolton, *War Eagle*, p. 69.
41	A player kicked a . . . ball on his helmet.: Bolton, *War Eagle*, p. 78.
41	The length of the halves . . . depended upon the weather.: Bolton, *War Eagle*, p. 80.
41	Teammates dragged a tackled ball carrier forward.: Bolton, *War Eagle*, p. 81.
41	Linemen held hands . . . before a play began.: Bolton, *The Crimson Tide*, p. 47.
41	handles were sewn . . . easier to toss.: Bolton, *War Eagle*, p. 81.
42	Strong, proud, and stubborn: *Game Day: North Carolina Basketball* (Chicago: Triumph Books, 2005), p. 9.
42	Actually a Horned Dorset Sheep,: "Rameses (mascot)," *Wikipedia, the free encyclopedia*, http://en.wikipedia.org/wiki/Rameses_(mascot), July 13, 2009.
42	since 1924 when cheerleader captain . . . rubbed Rameses' head for good luck.: *Game Day*, p. 9.
42	His life has had an overt . . . whose lives he touched.: Roger Rubin, "UNC Mascot Dies in Jersey," *New York Daily News*, March 27, 2007, http://www.nydailynews.com/sports/more_sports/2007/03/27/2007-03-27_unc_mascot_dies, July 13, 2009.
43	During a timeout, Quigg promised . . . deflected it to Tommy Kearns.: Fowler, p. 20.
43	In a Tar Heel practice before . . . Quigg never played again.: Fowler, p. 17.
44	He was a tuba player who . . . full-fledged freshman band member,": Mary E. Miller, "Time Marches On," *The News & Observer*, Sept. 8, 1995, http://us.mg2.mail.yahoo.com/dc/launch?.gx=1&.rand=830nk70uppvs8, Aug. 10, 2009.
44	I never saw a college . . . opportunity to play in one.: Miller.
45	Smith didn't often ask his players . . . was going exactly nowhere,": Fowler, p. 140.
45	"I had no idea what I . . . I agreed on the spot,": Fowler, p. 142.
45	While he first tried to . . . pizza he could find,: Fowler, p. 142.
46	when the Tar heel buses . . . before the scheduled 2 p.m. kickoff.: Rappaport, *Tar Heel: North Carolina Football*, p. 63.
46	Limping on an ankle injury suffered in the first quarter,: Rappaport, *Tar Heel: North Carolina Football*, p. 66.
46	"As soon as the ball hit . . . five minutes to clear the field,": Rappaport, *Tar Heel: North Carolina Football*, p. 64.
46	It was a real strange thing. . . . Nobody laid a hand on me.: Rappaport, *Tar Heel: North Carolina Football*, p. 63.
47	Williams was one of the most . . . loading up and spitting into the river.: Black with Fowler, p. 89.
48	they told Williams he wasn't . . . go to N.C. State instead.: Tim Stevens, "Donald Williams Serves a Dish of Critics Crow," *The News & Observer*, April 7, 1993, http://us.mg2.mail.yahoo.com/dc/launch?.

gx=1&.rand=3qlsitdj8n7pl, Aug. 7, 2009.

48   This highly recruited, high-scoring . . . shooting freshman in the country: Bryan Srickland, "From the Bench to the Limelight," *The Year in Review: 1993 National Champions* (Chapel Hill: *The Daily Tar Heel*, 1993), p. 10.

48   The 14-page UNC media guide's . . . to those who encouraged him: Strickland, p. 10.

49   the fastest goal in NCAA history: Rachel Carter, "Averbuch Gives Heels Good Shot," *The News & Observer*, Dec. 1, 2006, http://www.newsobserver.com/front/ story/516593.html, July 29, 2009.

49   Averbuch said she could boom . . . and 60 with her left.: Rachel Carter, "Record-Quick Goal Has Tar Heel in Spotlight," *The News & Observer*, Sept. 7, 2006, http:// www.newsobserver.com/sports/story/483444.html, July 29, 2009.

49   As a young player, she . . . alternating her feet.: Carter, "Averbuch Gives Heels Good Shot."

49   In pregame games, the Heels . . . to score a goal on it,": Carter, "Record-Quick Goal."

50   "was a cult sport." Adam Lucas, *The Best Game Ever* (Guilford, CT: The Lyons Press, 2006), p. 1.

50   "took the sport . . . than many of their competitors." Lucas, *The Best Game Ever*, p. 29.

50   When UNC's head basketball coach . . . barely anyone noticed.: Lucas, *The Best Game Ever*, p. 2.

50   The storyline was that the game . . . to move into the big time.: Lucas, *The Best Game Ever*, p. 40.

50   The rather prescient *Times* . . . as next year's NCAA champions.": Lucas, *The Best Game Ever*, p. 41.

51   No athlete in Carolina history . . . when he enrolled here.: .": Rappaport, *Tar Heel: North Carolina Basketball*, p. 195.

51   "best all-around player in the country.": .": Rappaport, *Tar Heel: North Carolina Basketball*, p. 196.

51   Scott decided to make the . . . for the sport he saw there.: .": Rappaport, *Tar Heel: North Carolina Basketball*, p. 202.

51   When he visited Chapel Hill, . . . felt like he belonged.": .": Rappaport, *Tar Heel: North Carolina Basketball*, p. 198.

51   "ugly racial threats" . . . certainly put him on the spot,": .": Rappaport, *Tar Heel: North Carolina Basketball*, p. 195.

51   It was pretty bad. . . . would be ashamed of it.": .": Rappaport, *Tar Heel: North Carolina Basketball*, p. 198.

52   who broke two tackles: Frank Heath, "Favorite Moments from Tar Heel Football History," *Tar Heel daily.com*, http://www.tarheeldaily.com/article.html?aid=1585, Aug. 7, 2009.

52   Lawrence hit one defender, . . . danced into the end zone.: Heath.

52   I think God made it simple. Just accept Him and believe.: Bettinger, p. 47.

53   one of the first persons . . . was one of his former teachers.: Robbi Pickeral, "Mixing Hoops with Hits," *The News & Observer*, June 15, 2007, http://www.newsobserver.com/front/story/604954.html, July 29, 2009.

53   Fox pursued his first love . . . hours I've ever spent ." Pickeral, "Mixing Hoops."

54   "we just picked up games as we could.": Rappaport, *Tar Heel: North Carolina Basketball*, p. 17.

54   In 1917, for example, a sign appeared . . . the squad and the training table.": Rappaport, *Tar Heel: North Carolina Basketball*, p. 24.

54   "Today's players would be lucky . . . people carried out on stretchers": Rappaport, *Tar Heel: North Carolina Basketball*, p. 26.

54   Tennent was widely recognized . . . couldn't dribble much.: Rappaport, *Tar Heel: North Carolina Basketball*, p. 26.

54   We played an aggressive . . . in the 30s and 40s.: Rappaport, *Tar Heel: North Carolina Basketball*, p. 26.

55   "his uncanny leaping ability.": Rappaport, *Tar Heel: North Carolina Basketball*, p. 165.

55   Cunningham earned his colorful . . . Duke player his freshman season.: Rappaport, *Tar Heel: North Carolina Basketball*, p. 170.

55   His sophomore season Cunningham . . . I've seen in a long time.": Rappaport, *Tar Heel: North Carolina Basketball*, p. 168.

55   "stood on pencil-thin legs . . . He was anything but poetry.": Rappaport, *Tar Heel: North Carolina Basketball*, p. 166.

55   Cunningham would consistently outjump players six inches taller.: Rappaport, *Tar Heel: North Carolina Basketball*, p. 168.

55   fitted neither Cunningham's size . . . his full opportunity in college.": Rappaport, *Tar Heel: North Carolina Basketball*, p. 170.

55   I could always jump.: Rappaport, *Tar Heel: North Carolina Basketball*, p. 166.

56   Before the third-largest crowd in Kenan Stadium history,: Robbi Pickeral, "Tar Heels Rally to Knock Off Irish," *The News & Observer*, Oct. 12, 2008, http://www.newsobserver.com/sports/story/1252288.html, July 28, 2009.

56   "It's a bitter ending," . . . recall a more bizarre game.: Caulton Tudor, "Justice Is Served for Tar Heels," *The News & Observer*, Oct. 12, 2008, http://www.newsobserver.com/sports/tudor/story/1252283.html, July 28, 2009.

56   None of us wants justice . . . we'd all go to hell.: Bettinger, p. 69.

57   Dean Smith's lot at the University of Kansas was as a sub.: Steve Elling, "Time to Sit and Learn," *The News & Observer*, March 16, 1997, http://docs.newsbank.com/s/InfoWeb/aggdocs/NewsBank/0EB035DC76ACEC06, Aug. 11, 2009.

57   Smith played for thirty seconds . . . until the game was decided.": Elling, "Time to Sit."

57   Smith was the prototypical coach: . . . cerebral side of the game.": Elling, "Time to Sit."

58   The double dip marked . . . and I just said 'Wow!'": Tom Harris, "The Good Times Return as Goalposts Come Down," *The News & Observer*, Oct. 25, 1992, http://docs.newsbank.com/s/InfoWeb/aggdocs/NewsBank/0EB03363917D5833, Aug. 10, 2009.

59   "It's a seniority thing," . . . who played here as a freshman.": Rappaport, *Tar Heel: North Carolina Basketball*, p. 218.

59   The 6'11"-McMillen publicly announced . . . reasons you know. Tom McMillen.: Rappaport, *Tar Heel: North Carolina Basketball*, p. 219.

59   "slender, soft-spoken giant": Rappaport, *Tar Heel: North Carolina Basketball*, p. 221.

60   twice running onto the field . . . on their way to touchdowns.: Rappaport, *Tar Heel: North Carolina Football*, p. 104.

60   on Saturday, Oct. 27, 1895, . . . the Georgia coach, Pop Warner.: Rappaport, *Tar Heel: North Carolina Football*, p. 105.

60   A squad of only fifteen players . . . players in the United States.": Rappaport, *Tar Heel: North Carolina Football*, p. 105.

61   Right next to pictures of his . . . "It was gushing. It was crazy.": Grant Wahl, "March Madman," *Sports Illustrated*, March 10, 2008, http://vault.sportsillustrated.ccn.com/vault/article/magazine/MAG1109933/index.htm, June 30, 2009.

61   "No player in memory has . . . moments in the lane": Wahl, "March Madman."

62   The Virginia game had become . . . an impassioned vendetta.": Rappaport, *Tar Heel: North Carolina Football*, p. 114.

62   administrators hired a new coach and allowed recruiting of players for the first time.: Rappaport, *Tar Heel: North Carolina Football*, p. 116.

62   Raby Tennent, recalled that the school . . . to start against Virginia to letter.: Rappaport, *Tar Heel: North Carolina Football*, p. 116.

62   A crowd of 15,000 was on hand: Rappaport, *Tar Heel: North Carolina Football*, p. 117.

62   Ecstatic fans carried the players around on their shoulders.:

Rappaport, *Tar Heel: North Carolina Football*, p. 114.

62   For the first time in history, . . . thinly disguised as Raby Bennett.: Rappaport, *Tar Heel: North Carolina Football*, p. 115.

63   He was so reliable and . . . that usually required several summers.: Adam Lucas, *Going Home Again* (Guilford, CN: The Lyons Press, 2004), pp. 42-43.

63   When the NCAA allowed . . . television shows across the state: Lucas, *Going Home Again*, p. 43.

63   and sold team calendars.: Lucas, *Going Home Again*, p. 44.

64   In April 1981, Streater was returning . . . the kind to be envied": Matt Ehlers, "A Fighter on the Field, and Beyond," *The News & Observer*, July 19, 2009, http://www. newsobserver.com/sports/college/unc/football/story/1613049.html, July 27, 2009.

64   Steve [Streater] lived life like we always think we should.: Ehlers.

65   "an exceptional basketball player . . . except from other coaches.": Steve Elling, "Calabria: A Carolina Character," *The News & Observer*, March 14, 1996. http://docs. newsbank.com/s/InfoWeb/aggdocs/NewsBank/0EB03537213ADDD5, Aug. 11, 2009.

65   "glamour guy," whose appearance . . . 25-gallon garbage can.: Elling, "Calabria: A Carolina Character."

65   Calabria looks more Hollywood than hardwood.: Elling, "Calabria: A Carolina Character."

66   Van, son of UNC women's . . . first women's basketball national championship.: Jeff Drew, "UNC Women Take First National Title," *The News & Observer*, April 4, 1994, http://docs.newsbank.com/s/InfoWeb/aggdocs/NewsBank/0EB0342406317D9E, Aug. 12, 2009.

66   the possession arrow pointed . . . officials switched it.: Drew.

66   "I knew as soon as . . . helping it come through.": Drew.

66   After he made his wish but . . . wash off into the water.": Drew.

67   Fretting that his players . . . heard regularly on the court.: Chansky, p. 131.

68   It was about as big as a family argument could get.": Rappaport, *Tar Heel: North Carolina Football*, p. 216.

68   "an unprecedented bowl matchup.": Rappaport, *Tar Heel: North Carolina Football*, p. 216.

68   "one of the most emotionally devastating matcups in college football.: Rappaport, *Tar Heel: North Carolina Football*, p. 216.

68   "strikingly similar . . . Jimmy Vickers, on his staff.": Rappaport, *Tar Heel: North Carolina Football*, p. 217.

68   "We never thought that we . . . against your brother's team.": Rappaport, *Tar Heel: North Carolina Football*, p. 216.

68   It was almost like playing against yourself.: Rappaport, *Tar Heel: North Carolina Football*, p. 217.

69   She has a gift . . . a loss for words.": A.J. Carr, "At UNC-CH, Another Berra Takes the Field," *The News & Observer*, Feb. 15, 1997, http://docs.newsbank.com/s/ InfoWeb/aggdocs/NewsBank/0EB035D2F1ABC907, Aug. 11, 2009.

69   without an athletic scholarship. . . . recreational ice hockey league.: Carr, "Another Berra."

69   who took no credit for . . . at the same time!": Carr, "Another Berra."

70   The decision was made to . . . in the final two minutes.: Chansky: p. 53.

70   As the Duke guard . . . corner of the Carolina bench.: Chansky, pp. 53-54.

70   It read "UNC 73 . . . score the Duke guard saw.: Chansky, p. 54.

70   The scorekeeper "cost us . . . Their scorekeeper did.": Chansky, p. 54.

71   I just knew we could do it.": Rappaport, *Tar Heel: North Carolina Football*, p. 185.

71   UNC was "housed in a plush . . . of mind to play football.": Rappaport, *Tar Heel: North Carolina Football*, p. 186.

71   "I had confidence all along," . . . a lot of scoring in that time.": Rappaport, *Tar Heel: North Carolina Football*, p. 185.

72   Let's do the things . . . we can still win.": Chansky, p. 137.

72 Smith ordered a trapping defense . . . with four seconds left.: Chansky, p. 137.

72 The shot hit back rim, . . . with three seconds left.: Chansky, p. 138.

72 Sophomore center Mitch Kupchak hit . . . the backboard through the hoop.: Chansky, p. 138.

72 the fans stormed the court. . . . I thought the game was tied.": Rappaport, *Tar Heel: North Carolina Basketball*, p. 239.

72 Wouldn't it be fun . . . being so far behind?: Chansky, p. 138.

73 under the new regime . . . 181 yards on 48 carries.: Peter King, "Out of the Carolina Blue," *Sports Illustrated*, Sept. 19, 2005, http://sportsillustrated.cnn.com/vault/article/magazine/MAG1112877/index.htm, Aug. 12, 2009.

73 the second undrafted back . . . more than 1,200 yards.: "Willie Parker," *Wikipedia, the free encyclopedia*, http://en.wikipedia.org/wiki/Willie_parker, Aug. 12, 2009.

73 If I had it to do . . . go to North Carolina.: King.

74 With 7:30 to go in the game . . . into the Four Corners offense.: Black with Fowler, p. 76.

74 Virginia countered by doing . . . the tournament record for fewest free throws.: Black with Fowler, p. 78.

74 "a monster of a controversy." Black with Fowler, p. 79.

74 "had an incredible impact . . . opposition to the slowdown.": Black with Fowler, p. 80.

74 "Our game at Virginia . . . think of it that way.": Black with Fowler, p. 81.

74 "I don't care if the score . . . have been a great win,": Black with Fowler, p. 79.

75 "next new great hope . . . as an eighth grader.": Caulton Tudor, "Former Quarterback Successful in Switch to Tight End at UNC," *The News & Observer*, Aug. 17, 1991, http://us.mg2.mail.yahoo.com/dc/launch?.gx=1&.rand=3qlsitdj8n7pl, Aug. 7, 2009.

75 "one of the most one-sided . . . high school because of injuries.: Tudor, "Former Quarterback."

75 "I lost confidence in myself . . . I just wanted to play.": Tudor, "Former Quarterback."

76 third-largest on-campus facility . . . shower heads are so high.": Curry Kirkpatrick, "Dingdong Duel in Dean's Dome," *Sports Illustrated*, Jan. 27, 1986, http://vault.sportsillutrated.cnn.com/vault/article/magazine/MAG1127172/index.htm, June 30, 2009.

76 Workmen were still climbing, . . . how noisy the place would be.: Kirkpatrick.

76 "If it's Duke-Carolina, it's the most intense rivalry of all time.": Kirkpatrick.

76 Hale spent the night . . . Anybody can make layups.": Kirkpatrick.

76 "one of the most formidable home-court advantages in the country.": "Dean Smith Center," *Wikipedia, the free encyclopedia*, http://en.wikipedia.org/wiki/Dean_Smith_Center, July 22, 2009.

76 This is one heck of a home-court advantage.: "Traditions," *2008-09 Carolina Basketball Media Guide*, p. 74. http://tarheelblue.cstv.com/auto/pdf/p_hotos/s_chools/unc/sports/m-baskbl/auto_pdf, July 23, 2009.

77 Deja voodoo: Alexander Wolff, "Technical Knockout," *Sports Illustrated*, April 12, 1993, http://vault.sportsillustrated.cnn.com/vault/article/magazine/MAG1138253/2/index.htm, June 30, 2009.

77 Early in the second half, . . . had to burn a timeout,": Wolff.

77 Lucky, yes. Fortunate, yes. But we're still NCAA champs.: *The Year in Review: 1993 National Champions* (Chapel Hill: *The Daily Tar Heel*, 1993), p. 27.

78 "When we came out of . . . didn't fare much better.: Rick Dorsey, "Tar Heels Recall 'Fog Bowl,'" *The News & Observer*, Dec. 28, 1995, http://docs.newsbank.com/s/InfoWeb/aggdocs/NewsBank/0EB0350D1412C870, Aug. 10, 2009.

78 Quarterbacks coach Steve Bryant remembered . . . there is by doing that.": Dorsey.

78 who had played for only two snaps: "1981 Gator Bowl," *Tar Heel*

	Football 1994, p. 109.
78	We played a good game, . . . talks about is the fog.: Dorsey.
79	Carolina was "in slow . . . new stars of the MTV era.": Chansky, p. 200.
79	"considered colossal basketball vessels . . . passing in the night.": Chansky, p. 200.
79	Dean Smith, however, knew what it . . . J.R. Reid and Scott Williams.: Chansky, p. 201.
79	"Ironically, it may have been . . . pull in tight on defense.: Chansky, p. 201.
80	had to fight his way through . . . That's how he got his players.": Rappaport, *Tar Heel: North Carolina Football*, p. 41.
80	That included Holdash's position . . . the best tackle on the team.: Rappaport, *Tar Heel: North Carolina Football*, p. 42.
80	On the third day of practice, . . . Tell your folks you're set here.": Rappaport, *Tar Heel: North Carolina Football*, pp. 42-43.
80	"despicable, vile, unprincipled scoundrels.": John MacArthur, *Twelve Ordinary Men* (Nashville: W Publishing Group, 2002), p. 152.
81	He was already a forward for . . . daughters are staunch Wolfpack fans.: Robbi Pickeral, "Mock Went Both Ways in Rivalry," *The News & Observer*, March 10, 2009, http://www.newsobserver.com/sports/college/story/1435783.html, July 28, 2009.
81	I felt sort of funny . . . my former teammates.: Pickeral, "Mock Went."
82	A New Yorker, he had taken . . . everybody returned the honor.": Frank Deford, "A Season of Change," *Sports Illustrated*, March 29, 1982, http://vault.sportsillustrated.cnn.com/vault/article/magazine/MAG1154821/index.htm, June 30, 2009.
82	"bush stuff." His office was . . . in a small apartment,: Deford, "A Season of Change."
82	they refused to institutionalize him.: "Biography: Frank McGuire, *Recognizing Greatness in High School Coaching*, March 2000, http://www.mcguirefoundation.org.about_us/frank_mcguirebio.htm, July 1, 2009.
83	After a civilized explanation of the . . . and flailed at each other.": Rappaport, *Tar Heel: North Carolina Football*, p. 88.
83	Football at UNC in those days . . . the matter at issue was settled.": Rappaport, *Tar Heel: North Carolina Football*, p. 95.
83	Each team had fifteen on a side, . . . nothing out of the ordinary had occurred.": Rappaport, *Tar Heel: North Carolina Football*, p. 96.
83	"barbarous affair.": Rappaport, *Tar Heel: North Carolina Football*, p. 88.
83	It was a rough game.: Rappaport, *Tar Heel: North Carolina Football*, p. 95.
84	What had the players looking . . . labeled simply "The Pit.": Lucas, Kirschner, and Bowers, p. 95.
84	The players went through their . . . No shooting, no dribbling, just defense.: Lucas, Kirschner, and Bowers, p. 98.
84	he was frustrated by the . . . going to make us successful.": Lucas, Kirschner, and Bowers, p. 180.
84	When the intense drills ended, . . . defensively in St. Louis.": Lucas, Kirschner, and Bowers, p. 98.
84	"were maybe our two best defensive games of the year.": Lucas, Kirschner, and Bowers, p. 136.
84	I think the Pit really helped us.: Lucas, Kirschner, and Bowers, p. 180.
85	"most controversial, debilitating, momentum-wrecking game": Steve Elling, "Heels Finally Rise from Ashes of '83," *The News & Observer*, Oct. 25, 1996, http://docs.newsbank.com/s/InfoWeb/aggdocs/NewsBank/0EB035A00E75D422 Aug. 11, 2009.
85	Facing them was a mob . . . into a "puzzling" skid.: Elling, "Heels Finally Rise."
85	I think people forget . . . No. 3 in the country.: Elling, "Heels Finally Rise."
86	Chancellor William Aycock conceded . . . was "virtually nonexistent.": Deford, "Long Ago."
86	Years later, Duke All-American . . . cheered for Smith to speak.: Deford, "Long

86   Ago."

      Coach Smith was a case of the right man at the right time.: Deford, "Long Ago."

87   Dorrance confessed he had to . . . a joyful place to compete from.": Eddy Landreth, "Winning It All Never Gets Old," *The News & Observer*, Dec. 10, 2008, http://www. newsobserver.com/print/wednesday/other/story/1328941.html, July 28, 2009.

87   "Right after they scored, we just went at them.": Landreth.

88   Only Utah State offered . . . brought him to Carolina.: Tim Layden, "Man of the Hour," *Sports Illustrated*, Sept. 22, 1997, http://vault.sportsillustrated.cnn.com/vault/ article/magazine/MAG 1010916/index.htm, June 30, 2009.

89   "when the 6-2 point guard . . . a hard time beating me.": Fowler, p. 106.

89   "Stan Rome elbowed me . . . kept his dribble alive, and kept on playing.": Fowler, p. 110.

90   On Sunday, March 24, 1957, . . . blared rousing Southern marches.": Gerald Holland, *Sports Illustrated*, as quoted by Adam Lucas, *The Best Game Ever*, p. 179.

90   In Chapel Hill, 2,000 people . . . until 2:00 a.m. to celebrate the win.: Lucas, *The Best Game Ever*, p. 180.

90   As the team flight neared . . . the airport to Chapel Hill,: Lucas, *The Best Game Ever*, p. 187.

90   the crowd swelled to an estimated 10,000 people.: Lucas, *The Best Game Ever*, p. 188.

90   "I don't think any of us . . . "It was extraordinary.": Lucas, *The Best Game Ever*, p. 187.

90   "crazy, but not riotous. . . . another crowd greeted them,": Lucas, *The Best Game Ever*, p. 188.

90   This is worse than V-J Day.: Lucas, *The Best Game Ever*, p. 180.

BIBLIOGRAPHY

"1981 Gator Bowl." *Tar Heel Football 1994: 1994 University of North Carolina Media Guide.* 208-09.

"1982 NCAA Champions." *2008-09 Carolina Basketball Media Guide.* 115. http://tarheelblue.cstv. com/auto/pdf/p_hotos/s_chools/unc/sports/m-baskbl/auto_pdf.

Ballard, Chris. "The Program." *Sports Illustrated on Campus.* 6 Nov. 2003. http://vault.sports illustrated.cnn.com/vault/article/web/COM1001589/index.htm.

Bechtel, Mark. "Great Briton." *Sports Illustrated.* 24 Dec. 2001. http://vault.sportsillustrated.cnn. com/vault/article/magazine/MAG1024608/index.htm.

"Before Kenan Stadium and Before Emerson Field." http://www.ramfanatic.com/Football/ before_kenan_stadium_and_before_.htm.

Bettinger, Jim & Julie S. *The Book of Bowden.* Nashville: TowleHouse Publishing, 2001.

"Biography: Frank McGuire." *Recognizing Greatness in High School Coaching.* March 2000. http:// www.mcguirefoundation.org/about_us/frank_mcguirebio.htm.

Black, Jimmy with Scott Fowler. *Jimmy Black's Tales from the Tar Heels.* Champaign, IL: Sports Publishing L.L.C., 2006.

Bolton, Clyde. *The Crimson Tide.* Huntsville, AL: The Strode Publishers, 1972.

---. *War Eagle.* Huntsville, AL: The Strode Publishers, 1973.

"Bromo-Seltzer." *Sour Stomachs and Galloping Headaches.* http://www.lib.unc.edu/ncc/ssgh/ strong.html.

Brown, David E. "Southern Beauty." *UNC General Alumni Association.* http://alumni.unc.edu/ article.aspx?SID=572.

"Carolina History." *2009 UNC Men's Lacrosse Media Guide.* 34-37. http://grfx.cstv.com/photos/ schools/unc/sports/m-lacros/auto_pdf/unc09-mlaxmg.pdf.

Carr, A.J. "At UNC-CH, Another Berra Takes the Field." *The News & Observer.* 15 Feb. 1997. http://docs.newsbank.com/s/InfoWeb/aggdocs/NewsBank/0EB035D2F1ABC907.

---. "Heels Win by a Little." *The News & Observer.* 25 Nov. 2007. http://www.newsobserver.com/ front/story/791984.html.

Carter, Rachel. "Averbuch Gives Heels Good Shot." *The News & Observer.* 1 Dec. 2006. http:// www.newsobserver.com/front/story/516593.html.

---. "Record-Quick Goal Has Tar Heel in Spotlight." *The News & Observer.* 7 Sept. 2006. http:// www.newsobserver.com/sports/story/483444.html.

Chansky, Art. *Blue Blood: Duke-Carolina: Inside the Most Storied Rivalry in College Hoops.* New York: Thomas Dunne Boooks, 2006.

"Charlie 'Choo-Choo' Justice." *Carolina Football: 2008 Media Guide.* http://tarheelblue.cstv.com/ sports/m-footbl/spec-rel/072708aaa.html.

Crothers, Tim. "Game of Choice." *Sports Illustrated.* 13 Aug. 2001. http://vault.sportsillustrated. cnn.com/vault/article/magazine/MAG1023179/index.htm.

"Dean Smith Center." *Wikipedia, the free encyclopedia.* http://en.wikipedia.org/wiki/Dean_ Smith_Center.

Deford, Frank. "Long Ago, He Won the Big One." *Sports Illustrated.* 29 Nov. 1982. http://vault. sportsillustrated.cnn.com/vault/article/magazine/MAG1126178/index.htm.

---. "A Season of Change." *Sports Illustrated.* 29 March 1982. http://vault.sportsillustrated.cnn. com/vault/article/magazine/MAG1154821/index.htm.

Dorsey, Rick. "Tar heels Recall 'Fog Bowl.'" *The News & Observer.* 28 Dec. 1995. http://docs. newsbank.com/s/InfoWeb/aggdocs/NewsBank/0EB0350D1412C870.

Drew, Jeff. "UNC Women Take First National Title." *The News & Observer.* 4 April 1994. http:// docs.newsbank.com/s/InfoWeb/aggdocs/NewsBank/0EB0342406317D9E.

Ehlers, Matt. "A Fighter on the Field, and Beyond." *The News & Observer.* 19 July 2009. http:// www.newsobserver.com/sports/college/unc/football/story/1613049.html.

Elling, Steve. "A Fullback's Moment of Glory." *The News & Observer.* 10 Oct. 1996. http://docs. newsbank.com/s/InfoWeb/aggdocs/NewsBank/0EB03599E8533E36.

---. "Calabria: A Carolina Character." *The News & Observer.* 14 March 1996. http://docs.news- bank.com/s/InfoWeb/aggdocs/NewsBank/0EB03537213ADDD5..

---. "Departing Deas Leaves His Mark." *The News & Observer*. 18 Aug. 1998. http://us.mg2.mail.
yahoo.com/dc/launch?.gx=1&.rand=3ic9flivb1geh.

---. "Heels Finally Rise from Ashes of '83." *The News & Observer*. 25 Oct. 1996. http://docs.news-
bank.com/s/InfoWeb/aggdocs/NewsBank/0EB035A00E75D422.

---. "Time to Sit and Learn." *The News & Observer*. 16 March 1997. http://docs.newsbank.com/s/
InfoWeb/aggdocs/NewsBank/0EB035DC76ACEC06.

Fowler, Scott. *North Carolina Tar Heels: Where Have You Gone?* Champaign, IL: Sports Publishing LLC, 2005.

Game Day: North Carolina Basketball. Chicago: Triumph Books, 2005.

Harris, Tom. "The Good Times Return as Goalposts Come Down." *The News & Observer*. 25
Oct. 1992. http://docs.newsbank.com/s/InfoWeb/aggdocs/NewsBank/
0EB03363917D5833.

"Head Coach Anson Dorrance." *2008 UNC Women's Soccer Media Guide*. 34-37. http://tarheel-
blue.cstv.com/auto_pdf/p_hotos/s_chools/unc/sports/w-soccer/auto_pdf/08-w-soccer-
mg.

Heath, Frank. "Favorite Moments from Tar Heel Football History." *Tar Heel daily.com*. http://
www.tarheeldaily.com/article/html?aid=1585.

Hynes, Warren. "A Comeback Made for Record Books." *The Year in Review: 1993 National
Champions*. Chapel Hill: *The Daily Tar Heel*, 1993. 34.

---. "A Season Built on Believing." *The Year in Review: 1993 National Champions*. Chapel Hill: *The
Daily Tar Heel*, 1993. 24-25.

King, Peter. "Out of the Carolina Blue." *Sports Illustrated*. 19 Sept. 2005. http://sportsillustrated.
cnn.com/vault/article/magazine/MAG1112877/index.htm.

Kirkpatrick, Curry. "Dingdong Duel in Dean's Dome." *Sports Illustrated*. 27 Jan. 1986. http://
vault.sportsillustrated.cnn.com/vault/article/magazine/MAG1127172/index.htm.

Landreth, Eddy. "Winning It All Never Gets Old." *The News & Observer*. 10 Dec. 2008. http://
www.newsobserver.com/print/wednesday/other/story/1328941.html.

Layden, Tim. "Man of the Hour." *Sports Illustrated*. 22 Sept. 1997. http://vault.sportsillustrated.
cnn.com/vault/article/magazine/MAG1010916/index.htm.

---. "Promise Fulfilled." *Sports Illustrated*. 15 April 2009. http://vault.sportsillustrated.cnn.com/
vault/article/magazine/MAG1154814/index.htm.

Lucas, Adam. *The Best Game Ever: How Frank McGuire's '57 Tar Heels Beat Wilt and Revolutionized
College Basketball*. Champaign, IL: The Lyons Press, 2006.

---. *Going Home Again: Roy Williams, the North Carolina Tar Heels, and a Season to Remember*.
Guilford, CN: The Lyons Press, 2004.

Lucas, Adam, Steve Kirschner, and Matt Bowers. *Led by Their Dreams: The Inside Story of
Carolina's Journey to the 2005 National Championship*. Guilford, CN: The Lyons Press,
2005.

MacArthur, John. *Twelve Ordinary Men*. Nashville: W Publishing Group, 2002.

Menez, Gene. "Danger: Highly Explosive." *Sports Illustrated*. 15 April 2009. http://vault.sports-
illustrated.cnn.com/vault/article/magazine/MAG1154819/index.htm.

Miller, Mary E. "Time Marches On." *The News & Observer*. 8 Sept. 1995. http://us.mg2.mail.
yahoo.com/dc/launch?.gx=1&.rand=830nk70uppvs8.

Pickeral, Robbi. "Mixing Hoops with Hits." *The News & Observer*. 15 June 2007. http://www.
newsobserver.com/front/story/604954.html.

---. "Mock Went Both Ways in Rivalry." *The News & Observer*. 10 March 2009. http://www.news-
observer.com/sports/college/story/1435783.html.

---. "Tar Heels Rally to Knock Off Irish." *The News & Observer*. 12 Oct. 2008. http://www.news-
observer.com/sports/story/1252288.html.

Quillin, Martha. "Town Loves Its Girl Latta." *The News & Observer*. 1 April 2006. http://www.
newsobserver.com/front/story/424211.html.

"Rameses (mascot)." *Wikipedia, the free encyclopedia*. http://en.wikipedia.org/wiki/
Rameses_(mascot).

Rappaport, Ken. *Tar Heel: North Carolina Basketball*. Huntsville, AL: The Strode
Publishers, 1976.

---. *Tar Heel: North Carolina Football.* Huntsville, AL: The Strode Publishers, 1976.

"Retired and Honored Jerseys at UNC: Charlotte Smith #23." *2008-09 UNC Women's Basketball Media Guide.* 104. http://tarheelblue.cstv.com/sports/w-baskbl/spec-rel/111308aae.html.

Rubin, Roger. "UNC Mascot Dies in Jersey." *New York Daily News.* 27 March 2007. http://www.nydailnews.com/sports/more_sports/2007/03/27/2007-03-27_unc_mascot_dies.

Stevens, Tim. "Donald Williams Serves a Dish of Critics Crow." *The News & Observer.* 7 April 1993. http://us.mg2.mail.yahoo.com/dc/launch?.gx=1&.rand=3qlsitdj8n7pl.

Strickland, Bryan. "From the Bench to the Limelight." *The Year in Review: 1993 National Champions.* Chapel Hill: *The Daily Tar Heel,* 1993. 10.

Taylor, Phil. "Shocking Blue." *Sports Illustrated.* 8 Nov. 2004. http://vault.sportsillustrated.cnn.com/vault/article/magazine/MAG1113619/index.htm.

"Traditions." *2008-09 Carolina Basketball Media Guide.* 64-86. http://tarheelblue.cstv.com/auto/pdf/p_hotos/s_chools/unc/sports/m-baskbl/auto_pdf.

Tudor, Caulton. "Fisher Hopes to Deliver On-Field Message, Too." *The News & Observer.* 22 Aug. 1998. http://us.mg2.mail.yahoo.com/dc/launch?.gx=1&.rand=3qlsitdj8n7pl.

---. "Former Quarterback Successful in Switch to Tight End at UNC." *The News & Observer.* 17 Aug. 1991. http://us.mg2.mail.yahoo.com/dc/launch?.gx=1&.rand=3qlsitdj8n7pl.

--- "Justice Is Served for Tar Heels." *The News & Observer.* 12 Oct. 2008. http://www.newsobserver.com/sports/tudor/story/1252283.html.

Ullrich, Rachel. "UNC's Gore a True Role Player." *The News & Observer.* 19 May 2009. http://www.newsobserver.com/sports/college/unc/story/1533227.html.

"UNC Kenan Stadium – 'America's Most Beautiful Stadium.'" http://www.sports-venue.info/NCAAF/Kenan_Stadium.html.

Wahl, Grant. "March Madman." *Sports Illustrated.* 10 March 2008. http://vault.sportsillustrated.ccn.com/vault/article/magazine/MAG1109933/index.htm.

"Why Tar Heels?" *Carolina Football: 2009 Football Media Guide.* 208. http://tarheelblue.cstv.com/sports/m-footbl/spec-rel/072809aab.html.

"Willie Parker." *Wikipedia, the free encyclopedia.* http://en.wikipedia.org/wiki/Willie_parker.

Wolff, Alexander. "Dean Emeritus." *Sports Illustrated.* 20 Oct. 1997. http://sportsillustrated.cnn.com/vault/article/magazine/MAG1011148/index.htm.

---. "No Question." *Sports Illustrated.* 16 Feb. 1998. http://sportsillustrated.cnn.com/vault/article/magazine/MAG10111982/index.htm.

---. "Technical Knockout." *Sports Illustrated.* 12 April 1993. http://vault.sportsillustrated.cnn.com/vault/article/magazine/MAG1138253/index.htm.

The Year in Review: 1993 National Champion. Chapel Hill: *The Daily Tar Heel,* 1993.

Yelton, Stephanie Lawrence. "1994 NCAA Championship Game: UNC 60, Louisiana Tech 59." *2008-09 UNC Women's Basketball Media Guide.* 100-01. http://tarheelblue.cstv.com/sports/w-baskbl/spec-rel/111308aae.html.

INDEX
(LAST NAME, DEVOTION DAY NUMBER)